W9-BBH-724

PAPER CRAFTS

Quick & Easy

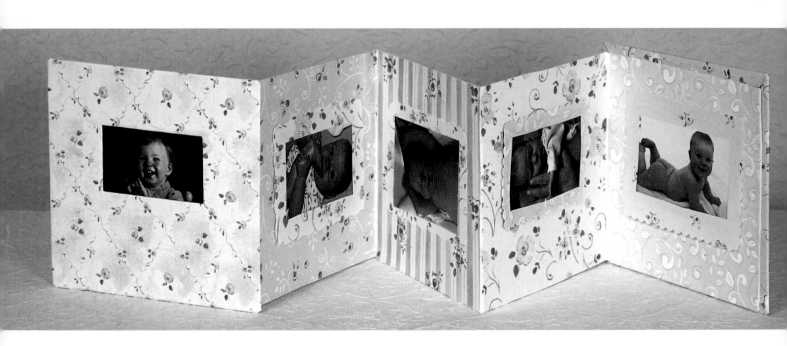

PAPER

Quick & Easy

CRAFTS

100
Fresh & Fun
PROJECTS
to Make

LARK
CRAFTS

An Imprint of Sterling Publishing Co., Inc.
New York

WWW.LARKCRAFTS.COM

Editor: Dawn Cusick
Art Director: Megan Kirby
Photography: Steve Mann, Evan Bracken
Contributing Writers: Kelly Banner, Cindy Burda,
  Valerie Van Arsdale Shrader, Kathleen Sheldon, and Terry Taylor
Cover Designer: Kristi Pfeffer
Illustrations: Orrin Lundgren and Shannon Yokeley
Art Assistance: Shannon Yokeley, Melanie Cooper,
  Biljana Bosevska, and Christopher Dollar

Library of Congress Cataloging-in-Publication Data

Quick & easy paper crafts : 100 fresh & fun projects to make. -- 1st ed.
    p. cm.
  Includes index.
  ISBN 978-1-60059-820-3 (pb-trade pbk. : alk. paper)
  1. Paper work. I. Lark Crafts (Firm) II. Title: Quick and easy paper crafts.
  TT870.Q44 2011
  745.54--dc22

                                  2010043268

10 9 8 7 6 5 4 3 2 1

Published by Lark Crafts
An Imprint of Sterling Publishing Co., Inc.
387 Park Avenue South, New York, NY 10016

First Paperback Edition 2011
Text © 2005, Lark Crafts, an Imprint of Sterling Publishing Co., Inc.; unless otherwise specified
Photography © 2005, Lark Crafts, an Imprint of Sterling Publishing Co., Inc.; unless otherwise specified
Illustrations © 2005, Lark Crafts, an Imprint of Sterling Publishing Co., Inc.; unless otherwise specified

Previously published as The Michaels Book of Paper Crafts

Distributed in Canada by Sterling Publishing,
c/o Canadian Manda Group, 165 Dufferin Street
Toronto, Ontario, Canada M6K 3H6

Distributed in the United Kingdom by GMC Distribution Services,
Castle Place, 166 High Street, Lewes, East Sussex, England BN7 1XU

Distributed in Australia by Capricorn Link (Australia) Pty Ltd.,
P.O. Box 704, Windsor, NSW 2756 Australia

If you have questions or comments about this book, please contact:
Lark Crafts
67 Broadway
Asheville, NC 28801
828-253-0467

Manufactured in China

ISBN 13: 978-1-57990-638-2 (hardcover) 978-1-60059-820-3 (paperback)

For information about custom editions, special sales, premium and corporate purchases,
please contact Sterling Special Sales Department at 800-805-5489 or specialsales@sterlingpub.com.

For information about desk and examination copies available to college and
university professors, requests must be submitted to academic@larkbooks.com.
Our complete policy can be found at www.larkcrafts.com.

contents

Introduction To Paper Crafts

The beginning of a book like this should, ideally, tell you a lot about paper—what types are available, their formal names, which craft projects they're perfect for, etc. (Don't worry; we'll get there, just turn the page.) Perhaps a better introduction to paper, though, is a much more personal one. Go to your local arts and crafts store and bask in the possibilities. Bring some of your favorites home and get to know them. Hold them up to the light. Touch them. Layer them. Fold them. See how well they hold a crease.

The popularity of scrapbooking and card making has fueled a huge demand and appreciation for unique papers. Vellums, embossed papers, handmade papers, embellished papers, novelty and vintage-print papers, and so much more are easy to find and (relatively) inexpensive. It's hard to imagine that paper crafters won't soon become notorious for hoarding large collections of paper they just "had to have."

If you love paper and paper crafts, this book is for you. You'll find ten project chapters, each providing illustrated techniques, a fun selection of projects, and a gallery for inspiration. Learn how to make scrapbook pages, journals, and handmade cards. Explore collage, decoupage, paper folding, and paper clay. Rediscover the fun of paper cutting, paper weaving, and paper mache. And learn how to create your own custom papers with simple surface design techniques.

So go shop for some great paper, then choose a project that's perfect for it and get started. The joy of crafting with paper awaits you!

7 must-have paper crafting materials & tools

paper!!!

Crafting paper can be divided into three basic weights, each of which offers certain benefits and drawbacks. Many projects in this book combine several paper types to maximize the best qualities of each.

Common lightweight papers include vellum and tissue papers. They're great for all types of layering, creating subtle effects with color and pattern. Many fine specialty papers (embroidered paper, lace paper, etc.) are also lightweight..

Popular medium-weight papers include most scrapbooking papers. These papers are suitable as backgrounds for many projects, as well as for folding projects.

Heavyweight papers such as corrugated cardboard, card stock, some embossed papers, and even some handmade papers provide a sturdy surface for embellishment. Their thickness often makes it difficult for them to hold a crease.

decorative-edged scissors

Decorative-edged scissors are one of those great craft tools whose novelty never seems to wear off, adding a fun sense of pizzazz to just about any paper craft project.

bone folders

Bone folders are used to smooth and flatten a variety of paper surfaces, from creases to recently glued surfaces.

eyelets & brads

Eyelets and brads now come in an amazing variety of shapes and colors. Use them as simple embellishments or to attach photographs, decorative papers, charms, or eyelet letters to your pages.

die-cut machines & paper punches

These relatively inexpensive machines are ideal for crafters looking for a more economical (and fun!) way to get larger cutout designs. For smaller die-cut patterns, a range of press and squeeze punches are available (See pages 204 through 241 for a variety of styles, projects, and more techniques.)

sticker machines

Sticker/lamination machines eliminate the wait for glue to dry, the worry about wrinkles, and the "goo" factor. Some machines create magnets and laminate as well as applying permanent or repositionable adhesive to paper, fabric, or other materials that are less than $1/16$ inch thick (1.6 mm).

Sticker/lamination machines are available in a small, sticker-sized, $1\frac{1}{2}$- inch-wide (4 cm) format, to the large format capable of applying adhesive to those 12-inch squares (30.5 cm) of designer scrapbook papers—or even a 12-inch wide continuous roll of paper! They're perfect for use with die-cutting machines, decorative punches, or to apply broad areas of colorful or patterned paper to your projects.

adhesives

The popularity of scrapbooking and card making has encouraged manufacturers to offer a great variety of adhesives.

Peel-and-stick mounting squares are an easy, no-mess way to attach photographs to paper.

Dimensional mounting tabs are a fun option for paper crafters, allowing you to create a three-dimensional look to your projects.

Basic craft glue is still a great adhesive choice, and is available in both liquid and stick forms. Just be sure to choose a clear-drying variety, and look for archival-safe glues when working with original photographs.

basic techniques

using a die-cut machine

1 Place your paper on the bed of the machine, aligning it as directed by the manufacturer.

2 Place your die-cut stamp on top of the paper, then bring the handle down in a smooth, firm motion.

3 Remove the paper from the machine, and gently separate your die-cut design from the paper.

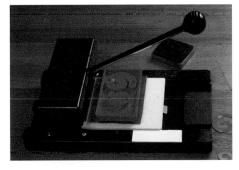

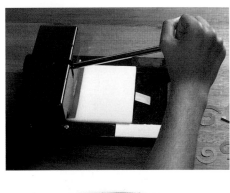

basic techniques

using a sticker machine

1 Trim your paper to no greater than the maximum width the machine allows.

2 Insert the paper into the machine and twist the handle until the paper comes out the opposite side.

3 Use your adhesive-backed paper as is, or, if you're feeling really adventurous, cut out fun sticker shapes with a die-cut machine or a paper punch.

using brads

To use a brad, make a small hole on the right side of your paper with a paper piercing tool or embroidery needle. Press the closed brad into the hole, open the wings on the back side of the paper, and press to secure in place.

using a bone folder

To use a bone folder, simply move it down a folded crease or other paper surface you'd like to smooth, pressing firmly but gently.

tearing paper

Put away the scissors and try tearing to add texture and spontaneity to your designs. You can (with a little practice) learn to let 'er rip! To get the straightest edge (and most control) when tearing, tear with the grain of the paper against a straight edge (such as a ruler). For a less rigid tear, crease the paper with the grain of the paper and smooth with a bone folder, then unfold and tear.

Many papers develop a white edge, called the chamfered edge, when torn. Sometimes this edge is desired—shapes with a chamfered edge will stand out better against a background. If you don't want the white edge, put both thumbs on either side of where you start the tear. The edge you pull toward you will not be chamfered. Another option is to disguise the white edges by lightly brushing them with colored chalk.

basic techniques

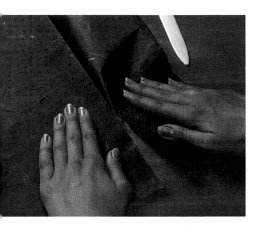

using eyelets

1 Place the paper you'll be adding the eyelet to on a piece of cardboard or an old magazine. Use a pencil to lightly mark the paper where you want to add the eyelet.

2 Use the punch end of the eyelet setting tool to make a hole at the pencil mark by hitting the top of the tool with a small hammer.

3 Push the eyelet through the hole so that its front side is on the front side of the paper. (If you want to use the eyelet to attach something to the paper, push it through that item first.)

4 Turn the paper over so the front of the eyelet is facing down. To anchor the back of the eyelet in place, first match the eyelet setting tip to the size of your eyelet.

5 Position the tool over the eyelet, and hit the back of the setting tool with a small hammer.

Testing the Grain of Your Paper

The grain of your paper often tells you how easily the paper will fold. Handmade paper may not have a discernible grain, but machine-made papers will; it corresponds to the direction the paper moved during its manufacture. To test the grain, fold the paper both vertically and horizontally, but don't crease it. The paper may be more flexible in one direction, which is parallel to the grain. The more pronounced the difference between the vertical and horizontal folds, the more difficult it will be to use the paper successfully. Generally, the thicker the paper, the harder it is to fold against the grain.

Another way to test the grain is to tear the paper. Cut a sample square of the paper, and rip it forcefully from top to bottom. The paper will tear easily in a fairly straight line if you've ripped it along the grain. If the paper is hard to rip and the tear line is frayed and uneven, you've torn it against the grain.

Scrapbooking

What better way to indulge your whimsical side than by playing with paper cutting, punching, and piercing? The techniques are incredibly simple, and the results can be spectacular, letting you dress up everything from scrapbooking pages to handcrafted cards to gift bags.

materials

albums

Today's albums run the gamut in terms of both style and size. When choosing albums, consider the amount of material you'll be presenting, your subject matter, and how the album will be used. Remember, you may want to move or add pages in the future, so be sure the pages are both removable and sturdy.

miniatures

Soccer balls, birthday cakes, lettering, and baby buggies—just about anything you can imagine can be found in miniature. The hard part will be limiting your selection so these decorations enhance, rather than overwhelm, your design.

papers

Forget those plain dark pages of your grandmother's scrapbooks! A dazzling selection of papers is now available: marbled, sueded, embossed, metallic, textured, and faux finishes, to name just a few. If you have trouble choosing, bring your photos and mementos to the craft store to find the perfect match.

vellum

This translucent paper, which comes in many different patterns and colors, adds dimension and texture to your pages. Use ink, chalk, or paint to write on vellum.

embellishments

Buttons from a favorite dress, postage stamps, beads, charms, decorative trim, and fabric flowers are just a few of the ornaments you can use to adorn your pages.

stamps & stickers

Even if you aren't an accomplished artist, you can still add terrific-looking art or text to the pages and covers of your scrapbooks, thanks to the ease of stamps and stickers. Available in a wide range of styles, from elegant to playful, stamps and stickers are a simple way to dress up your memory books.

memorabilia pockets

Use pockets to tuck special letters, tags, and trinkets away for future generations to discover.

wire

Both colored and metallic wire can be manipulated into various shapes to add an eye-catching enhancement to your album pages.

decorative punches & die cuts

Decorative punches (hole punches that cut fun shapes) are a quick way to add pizzazz to your papers. Die-cut images, available in craft stores, can be found to suit practically any theme.

adhesives

Read labels to find the best match for your various materials, and make sure the adhesives you choose are labeled "acid free." Also, consider adding one of the new home laminating machines to your crafting tool collection. These machines can attach a permanent or repositionable adhesive to the back sides of most papers in under a minute.

Choosing Papers

Too many wonderful papers to choose just one? Layering different background papers creates a wonderful effect for your scrapbooking pages.

Take your photographs with you to the store to help you select papers that enhance, rather than detract from, your pictures. Play with pattern, color, and thickness. Transparent vellums will add an extra dimension to your layering possibilities.

basic techniques

choosing & cropping photos

Most scrapbooking pages feature a large focal photo. For maximum impact, the important areas in the photo should be colorful and in focus. Creative cropping can also add pizzazz to your pages by removing visual "clutter," as well as drawing the viewer's attention to unusual areas in the photo.

1 Measure and cut a ¼- to ½-inch (6 to 13 mm) border on the inside of a piece of paper. Cut this into two L shapes.

2 Arrange the two L shapes on the photo to test various cropping possibilities. When you've found the best position, lightly mark the new corners with a pencil.

making borders for photos

Borders can be made from items such as greeting cards and doilies or from purchased templates. Just about any photo will benefit from one of these frames.

1 To make your own border, simply mark the cutting lines for your photo's opening on your paper with a ruler or other straightedge, then use a craft knife to cut out a photo window. Change to a new blade if needed to get a clean edge. An easy alternative is to mount your photo directly onto a piece of background paper, then trim off just enough of the excess paper to leave an interesting background. NOTE: Incredible borders in every color and pattern can be found pre-made in scrapbooking sections of craft stores.

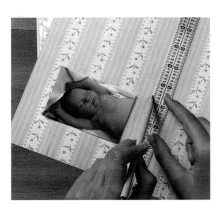

Making Memories

Gathering the scraps that make up a scrapbook (photos, mementos, newspaper clippings, dates, names, and embellishments) is really a matter of getting into the habit of collecting and organizing the "stuff" of memories. Keep all the items you'd like to include in your scrapbooks in a convenient place, and write down any important information (dates, ages of children, photo captions, and place names) while it is still fresh in your mind. Ask friends and family members if they have photos to share (you can have copies or color photocopies made).

While it's always nice to have a record of big events such as childbirth, graduations, weddings, travel, birthdays, and anniversaries, it's also often the little things that make for wonderful memories: the funny thing your five-year-old said as you were tucking him in one night, the afternoon you spend chatting with

(continues on following page)

basic techniques

your great-aunt on her porch. Get in the habit of collecting small mementos (a lock of your child's hair, a blossom from your aunt's window box) to help preserve these special moments in memory.

Store your items in envelopes or shoe boxes with careful notations to help you remember dates, names, etc. Once you get started thinking beyond the conventional photos, programs, and ticket stubs, you'll find yourself automatically squirreling away the scrap of fabric, the stub of your child's favorite blue crayon, the radio knob that finally fell off when your beloved car's odometer hit 170,000 miles.

2 To make a border using a purchased template, choose the paper for your border and then place the template on the paper and trace the desired shape. Use a craft knife to cut out the shape. Remove the cut paper, and then position the frame over your photo.

3 You can dress up your borders with decorative-edged scissors or hole punches.

4 If desired, create multiple border layers for your photos, creating contrast with color and pattern.

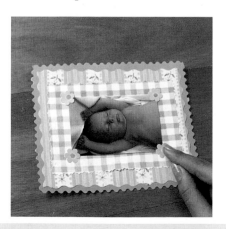

5 A fun option, especially for vintage photos, is to make a "shadow border" on one side of the photo.

3-D Memories

Start to explore the craft of memory making, and you'll discover the world of scrapbooking is no longer flat. Today's albums and pages are made to accommodate all manner of mementos and embellishments.

Many larger items can be attached to a scrapbooking page with glue or wire. If the item's weight causes the page to buckle, glue a supportive layer (cut slightly smaller than the page on all sides) of poster board or card stock to the back of the scrapbooking page. Display in a frame or in an open book.

typography

It's true that a picture is worth a thousand words, but a little text can enhance your design and help turn your scrapbook into a family heirloom.

Look around and you'll realize that letters are everywhere. You can purchase peel-and-stick or press type letters, use rubber stamps, or cut letters from magazines or even food cartons. Your computer will also provide a variety of fonts and sizes. Don't feel that you have to follow the old, line-'em-up-straight rule: Play around with your letters, slanting them up or down the page or even scattering them about to create playful effect.

You can also create great special lettering effects on your home computer. You can just type the headline you want and format it in your favorite font, if you like, or create a random lettering effect by giving individual letters different formatting treatments.

chalking

Perhaps the most fun in scrapbooking is the continual discovery of new products and techniques. Colored chalks are inexpensive to purchase and make it easy to add hints of color and shading to your favorite pages.

decorating with charms

Charms make wonderful decorative additions to scrapbook pages, and they're a cinch to attach.

To attach a charm, first use a hole piercer to poke two small holes in the paper.

Thread thin-gauge wire through the charm, and then thread the wire through both holes. Twist both ends of the wire on the back side of the paper to hold the charm in place. Any excess wire can be trimmed with wire cutters.

Current Events

Remember that scrapbooking is about both the past and the future. The headlines of our day will be tomorrow's history, and your children's children will treasure your personal views of the world. Supplement newspaper and magazine clippings about current events with your own personal reactions. Keep a journal where you record your thoughts about what's happening in the world. How does it affect your daily life, or the lives of those close to you? What are your predictions for the future? Find headlines, quotations, and even cartoons that express your feelings about major events.

Wedding Day

Stems of purple lilac in the bride's bouquet inspired the lavender color palette of this scrapbooking page. The triple border design running down the side of the page is ideal for showcasing close-up photos or fun embellishments.

Designer: Beth Berutich

materials

Sheet of decorative paper for background

Sheet of white paper

1 sheet each of coordinating decorative paper and vellum

Wedding photo

Wedding dress embellishments

Adhesive photo squares

Metallic photo corners

Sticker letters

Narrow ribbon

step by step

1 For the embellishment borders, cut three 1¾-inch (4.5 cm) squares from the white paper, three 2-inch (5 cm) squares from the nonbackground decorative paper, and three 3-inch (7.5 cm) squares from the vellum.

2 Tip the white squares on their diagonal and adhere your embellishment. Attach the white squares to the 2-inch decorative paper squares, then attach those squares to the vellum squares. Attach each of these squares down the side of the background paper.

3 To create the photo borders, cut a piece of the nonbackground decorative paper that's 1 inch (2.5 cm) larger on all sides than your photograph, then cut a piece of white paper that's ⅛ inch (3 mm) larger on all sides than the decorative paper. Attach the photo to the borders, then position and attach it to the background paper. Position and adhere decorative photo corners in place.

4 To create the title box, cut 1¾- x 3⅜-inch (4.5 x 8.5 cm) and 2¼- x 6⅞-inch (5.75 x 17.5 cm) rectangles from the white paper, a 1¾- x 4-inch (4.5 x 10 cm) rectangle from the vellum, and a 2- x 6¾-inch (5 x 17 cm) rectangle from the nonbackground decorative paper.

5 Spell out your chosen title with sticker letters on the smaller white rectangle. Attach a length of narrow ribbon to the back side of the rectangle, allowing it to protrude as much as desired. Trim the ribbon ends at an angle.

6 Attach the white rectangle to the vellum, then mount that on the nonbackground decorative paper. Center and attach the bordered text block onto the second white rectangle to create a narrow white border, then position and adhere to the background paper.

tip *Add personal touches to your wedding pages by including mementos from the wedding such as pressed petals from the bouquet, an invitation, or even a small piece of lace from the dress.*

Family Time

Today's high-quality color photocopiers make scrapbooking with old family photos easier and more fun than ever. When photocopying old black and white photos, always reproduce them in color to capture any sepia tones or discoloration from aging.

Designer: Beth Berutich

materials

Faux wood grain background paper

Floral ribbon stamp

Clear ink pad

Color photocopy of a family photo

Dark brown paper

Adhesive mounting squares

Vellum

Gold, brown, yellow, and orange chalk

Copper eyelets

Eyelet setting tool

Cream ribbon

Brown suede or felt scraps

Cameo embellishments or shank buttons

Brown marker

Tacky tape

Glue gun

step by step

1 To create an aged, faux wallpaper look to your background paper, stamp vertical rows of designs with the clear ink about every 2 inches (5 cm) across the paper.

2 Mount your photo onto the dark brown paper. Trim to create a narrow border.

3 Hold the vellum over your framed photo, then measure and mark a 1-inch-wide (2.5 cm) border that will overlap the photo.

4 Tear the edges of the vellum border, cutting a large X in the center area to make it more accessible. Age the vellum frame by rubbing gold, brown, yellow, and orange chalks over the vellum's rough edges.

5 Position the vellum frame over the mounted photo, then secure the layers to the background paper with eyelets.

6 Cut a length of ribbon to the height of your scrapbooking page plus 4 inches (10 cm). Age the ribbon with chalk until you're happy with the effect.

7 Cut ovals of suede or felt, and secure them to the ribbon with double-sided tape, referring to the photo as a guide. Secure the cameos to the center of the ovals with hot glue. Add sticker letters or numbers to finish.

Most Wanted Baby

For text ideas, the designer of this creative page visited the FBI's Most Wanted website, then adapted their categories to details from her baby's world. "Considered Armed with a Flannel Blanket and Extremely Dangerous" is one of the fun results of that research!

materials

Neutral background paper

Focal photo

Sheet of brown card stock

Adhesive tabs

Sheet of brown faux suede paper

Self-adhesive mesh

Small piece of hemp cord

Paper piercing tool

Neutral colored vellum

Brown chalk

Metal eyelets

Computer and printer

step by step

1 Mount your focal photo on a piece of card stock and trim to leave a narrow border. Mount the photo on the background paper.

2 Trim narrow strips from the brown suede paper, and attach them to the corners, referring to the photo as a guide.

3 Cut two rectangles of adhesive mesh and place one on each side of the background paper, referring to the photo as a guide. Use a paper piercing tool or embroidery needle to work a short length of hemp into the top center of each mesh rectangle. Knot the hemp on the front side and trim.

4 Type the "vital statistics" and Most Wanted headline on a computer. Print them out on a sheet of vellum. Tear the areas around the text, then brush them with brown chalk. Attach the vellum to the mesh.

5 Attach the Most Wanted vellum to the background paper with eyelets.

Create striking effects blending black and white photographs with black, white, and gray scrapbooking papers.

BRADLEY
ALEXANDER
BERUTICH

DESCRIPTION:

WEIGHT: 22 POUNDS

HEIGHT: 30 INCHES

HAIR: BROWN

EYES: BLUE

TEETH: 2 BOTTOM
          1 UPPER

REMARKS:

MOMMYS BOY

COMMANDO CRAWLER

WAVES BYE BYE

PULLS TO STANDING

EXAMINES HANDS

SHAKES HEAD NO NO!

SAYS DA DA DA

PEEK A BOO EXPERT

MOST WANTED

CONSIDERED ARMED WITH FLANNEL BLANKET
AND EXTREMELY DANGEROUS

Designer: Beth Berutich

Designer: Chris Rankin

Holiday Memories

Ever wonder what to do with all of those snapshots you've taken of loved ones opening their holiday gifts? Wrap them up as packages, of course, then arrange them under a decorated Christmas tree to create a festive scrapbooking page.

materials

Photographs

1 sheet each of red, green, and gold background papers

2 sheets decorative holiday papers

Scrap paper

Holiday stickers and scrapbooking embellishments

Red and gold embroidery floss, string, or narrow ribbon

Pencil and ruler

Adhesive photo mount squares

Clear-drying craft glue

step by step

1 Make color photocopies of your holiday pictures, enlarging or reducing as needed so you have at least one large and two small photos.

2 Trim the photocopies, then mount the larger photo on one of your decorative papers and the smaller photos on the gold paper. Cut around the mounted photos to create borders in the desired size.

3 Attach your mounted large photo to your back-ground paper, tilting it at an angle if desired. Cut a strip of decorative holiday paper for the bottom of the page, referring to the photo as a guide. Attach the strip to the background paper with glue.

4 To make the Christmas tree, fold your scrap paper in half and sketch half a triangle on it. Cut out the shape, then open the paper and position it on the right side of your page. Make any necessary adjustments in size or shape, then use the scrap paper as a pattern to cut out a tree from the green paper. Attach the tree to the background paper.

5 Cut short lengths of red floss, string, or narrow ribbon and arrange them on the tree for garland. Secure them in place on each side of the tree with a dab of glue. Decorate the tree with holiday stickers and/or embellishments.

6 Arrange your smaller pho-tographs under the tree and secure in place with glue or adhesive squares. Tie short lengths of gold floss, string, or narrow ribbon into bows and glue them to the tops of your packages photographs.

7 Tie two short lengths of red floss, string, or nar-row ribbon into bows and glue them to the bottom corners of the page.

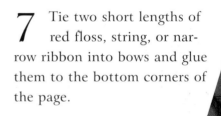

Play On!

The incredible range of scrapbooking papers available today includes such novel products as the printed sports ball paper used in this project. Add photos of your favorite little sports star and some great lettering, and you have a fabulous page in less than an hour.

Designer: Martha Teater

materials

Photographs

Sheets of sports scrapbooking
  paper

2 sheets of medium-weight paper,
  one solid green and one solid
  black

Scrap of white paper

Novelty metal die-cut letters

Novelty scrabble letters

Pencil and ruler

Adhesive photo mount squares

Clear-drying craft glue

step by step

1 Make color photocopies
  of your sports pictures,
enlarging or reducing as needed
so you have at least one vertical, one horizontal, and one
square photo.

2 Trim the photocopies,
  then mount the horizon-
tal and vertical photos on
green paper. Trim the vertical
photo to create a narrow green
border, then trim the horizontal photo with a wider border,
leaving 2 inches (5 cm) on the
right side (see photo). Double-
mount the vertical photo on
black paper, trimming to create
a 1-inch (2.5 cm) border on
the left side (see photo).

3 Mount the square photo
  on a piece of black paper,
then trim to create a narrow
border on the side and bottom
edges and a ¾-inch (18 mm)
border at the top.

4 Attach all three mounted
  photos to the soccer
paper, referring to the photo as
a guide.

5 Spell out your sports
  star's name in novelty letters down the left side of the
top photo.

6 Cut out a narrow rectangle to fit on the top
edge of the square photo's
border. Secure it in place,
then spell out "ATTACK" in
scrabble letters.

7 Arrange more scrabble
  letters on the green border of the bottom photo to
spell out "SOCCER MEN."

Batter up! Let the great selection of sports papers guide your creativity. The
"Play Ball" lettering was created on a computer, then printed out and mounted
on background paper.
Designer: Chris Rankin

Scrapbooking Gallery

Great things can happen when you venture out of the scrapbooking aisle every once and a while. The faux dog leash was made with trim from the leather department, while the letters in the dog tag were created with a leather embossing tool. Designer: Beth Berutich

Collage is a great technique for scrapbookers. The finished pages are striking and it's a great way to use up some of those great paper scraps you've accumulated.
Designer: Beth Berutich

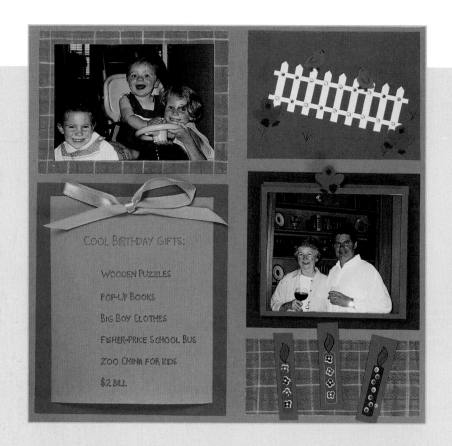

Left and above: Too many photos, too little space? Add an interactive element to your scrapbooking pages with a fold-out photo display. Designer: Beth Berutich

Left: Often a single, large photo makes a great page. The letters were mounted on squares and then tied into a vertical banner with leather cording. Designer: Beth Berutich

Right: Two-page spreads are a fun way to display related scrapbooking pages. In the page above, a pocket was created to hold special birthday cards and momentos. The page at right features photos of the birthday girls and their presents.
Designer: Beth Berutich

Left: Celebrate your garden blooms with a scrapbooking page of your favorite flowers displayed in vellum envelopes. Designer: Beth Berutich

Left: Halloween costume photos make great scrapbooking pages. The Trick or Treat tags in this page are decorated with elements from the kids' costumes. Designer: Beth Berutich

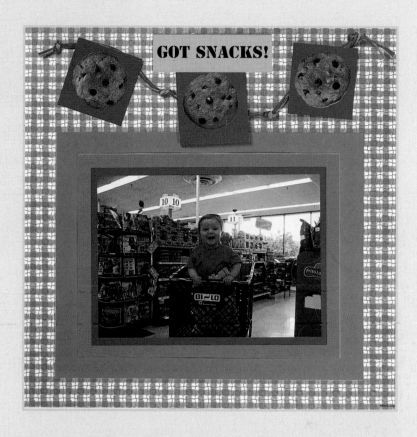

Right: Looking for inspiration? Pop culture phrases and icons are a great way to capture the spirit of the times and prod your imagination. Designer: Beth Berutich

Right: The twinkling glitter photo frame matches the glitter in his eyes! The left side of the page provides room to showcase the many moods of a baby. Designer: Beth Berutich

Why keep your best scrapbooking pages in between the pages of an album? A simple gradeschool photo was arranged on a collage of background papers and framed for a wall hanging.
Designer: Stephanie Inman

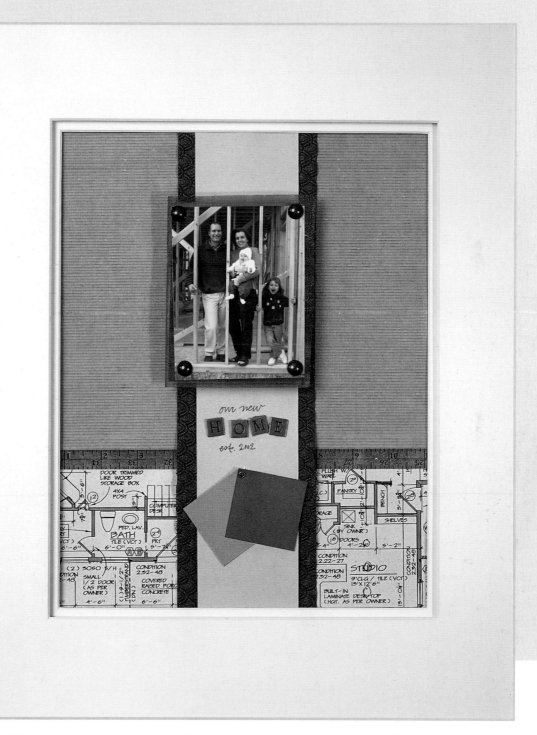

The building of a house was documented using a blend of materials from the building process and the scrapbooking aisle.
Designer: Stephanie Inman

Card Making

Perhaps no gesture makes more of an impact than presenting a handmade, heartfelt card. Making your own cards can be one of the most rewarding crafting experiences, with an endless variety of materials and techniques to explore. Find a special paper to stamp, stencil, stitch, emboss, or collage, then add eyelets, beads, ribbon, found objects, even computer-generated imagery to create your own unique keepsake cards.

Mr. and Mrs. Jimmy Sweet
have the honour of announcing
the marriage of their daughter
Ivy Mae
to
Andrew Thomas Millon

materials

paper

The most important supply for making cards, paper is available in an endless variety of colors, patterns, textures, and weights. For greatest longevity, choose an archival paper.

adhesives

Select the adhesive most appropriate for your project: common white craft glue (PVA, or polyvinyl acetate) dries clear so it works quite well for card making, where appearance is utmost. Glue sticks, spray adhesive, decoupage medium, double-sided tape, and hot glue can be used, too.

craft knife

Since you'll need to make any number of precise cuts, keep a sharp craft knife on hand. Replace the blades often for best results.

cutting mat

A self-healing cutting mat protects your work surface, and the grid is helpful when cutting to precise measurements.

metal ruler

Use a metal ruler not only for measuring, but also as a straightedge for scoring and cutting.

scissors

Papers cut with decorative-edged scissors add a lot of visual interest to cards and collage materials. Of course, you'll need a pair of sharp household scissors, too.

hole & shaped punches

Craft punches create a variety of interesting shapes for collage and can be used to make negative space in a larger piece of paper. The common one-hole punch is also helpful.

bone folder

This inexpensive tool is indispensable to card making, as it helps form crisp folds. It is also important when burnishing together glued elements.

stamps, stencils, & more

Virtually any technique can be used to embellish cards, such as rubber stamping, stenciling, painting, embossing, and collaging. Gather up the craft supplies you have on hand to use when you are making cards.

decorative elements

The sky's the limit: craft wire, bits of fabric, scraps of paper, eyelets, beads, buttons, natural materials, ribbon, found objects, foils—the list is endless!

Make Your Own Envelope

It's surprisingly simple to make your own custom envelopes for your handmade cards. The formula is that the central rectangle or square of the envelope should be approximately ⅛ to ⅜ inch (3 mm to 1 cm) larger than the card. For the patterns given here, simply fold the two side flaps in and the bottom flap up, scoring and sharpening each fold with a bone folder. Glue the bottom flap in place. Lastly, score and fold the top flap over, again using the bone folder.

Here's another tip: if you receive a card in an envelope that you like, simply take it apart to see how it's designed! Then you can re-create the style for your own cards.

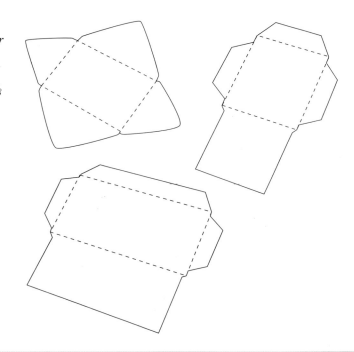

basic techniques

gluing & burnishing

This simple method should be used regardless of the type of glue you use, whether a spray, a stick, or a liquid, because it ensures that your elements will bond properly to your card.

1 Lay the piece of paper you'll be gluing wrong side up on a scrap piece of paper, so the side to be adhered is facing up. Apply your adhesive over the entire paper surface, being sure to extend past the edges. When you've applied the adhesive, pick up the piece with the tip of your finger or the end of a craft knife and place it on the card.

2 Burnish to seal the bond between the glued piece and the dry card. Place a piece of waxed paper over the surface you just glued and press firmly along the entire area with a bone folder. The waxed paper

allows you to see the card while you're burnishing and protects the card, too, because the bone folder can cause the paper to become shiny as it breaks the fibers on the surface of the card.

3 For maximum adhesion, you may want to press the card between the pages of a heavy book. Keep it covered with waxed paper as it dries.

NOTE: Use a fresh sheet of scrap paper each time you glue to keep glue from transferring onto your card paper.

Will Your Card Survive the Mail?

Absolutely, as long as you take the necessary steps to protect your special, one-of-a-kind creation. Because hand-made cards are often made with bulky or heavy materials and may be in an envelope that is an unconventional size, you should take the extra effort to pro-tect your card. An extra layer of paper wrapped around the card before placing in an envelope can make all the differ-ence. It's wise to take your cards to the post office so each item can be properly weighed and stamped as "fragile." Your card—call it mail art if you want—may require additional postage.

making a blank card

Although blank cards are readily available, you have complete creative control when you make your own, because you can design every detail, choosing the type of paper and the size.

1 After you've decided on the size of your card, cut a piece of card stock that meas-ures twice that size. For exam-ple, to make a 4- x 5-inch (10 x 12.5 cm) card, cut a piece of card stock that is 8 x 5 inches (20 x 12.5 cm). If you plan to insert your card in a premade

basic techniques

Sewing on Cards

Don't neglect your sewing basket when you are making cards. You can attach elements or add interesting details to your cards by stitching on them, either by hand or by machine. Use sewing thread, embroidery floss, or specialty threads such as metallics to add pizzazz to your projects.

When you stitch paper by hand, it's generally preferable to pierce the holes with a larger needle first, then add the stitching, to prevent tears and rough edges. When you're done, cover the knots on the back side of the card with a piece of decorative paper or a sticker. See pages 278 and 279 for complete instructions.

You can also use your sewing machine to collage paper together, stitch elements to the face of the card, or simply provide a decorative touch. Be sure to use a long running stitch or a wide zigzag, because short tight stitches may tear the paper. If you prefer, you can also lower the feed on your machine and turn the wheel by hand to stitch slowly.

envelope, your card should be approximately 1/8 to 3/8 inch (3 to 9 mm) smaller than the envelope so it slides in easily.

2 On the inside of the card stock, lightly mark the midpoint. Place a metal ruler along this midpoint and use a bone folder to score along this line from one end to the other. Scoring breaks the top layer of the paper fibers and makes it easier to create a crisp fold.

3 Fold the card in half along the scored line. To sharpen the fold, press slowly yet firmly along the fold with the curved edge of the bone folder.

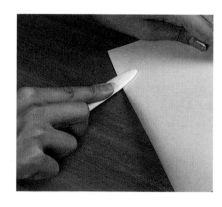

NOTE: To add a decorative border to your card, cut the front edge with a pair of decorative-edged scissors or tear it against a deckle-edged ruler.

cutting windows

So simple to make, a window allows you to create special effects and add exciting imagery such as photographs and photocopies.

1 Measure and mark the area for the window on the front side of your card.

2 Cut out the window with a sharp craft knife, switching to a new blade if your cuts aren't clean and smooth.

3 If desired, layer a border (or multiple borders) on the inside of the card to show through the window.

making multilayered cards

Multilayered cards are a great way to showcase specialty papers such as vellums. Choose papers that are distinctly different in color and texture for best effect.

1 To make a multilayered card, first make multiple blank cards with the same dimensions. Pierce holes about an inch (2.5 cm) from the edges of the fold line at top and bottom.

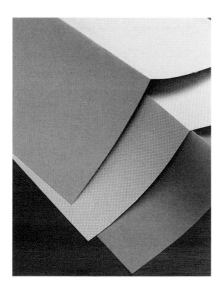

2 Align the cards so their right sides face up, then thread an embroidery needle with 12 inches (30 cm) of ribbon, yarn, colored wire, or embroidery floss. Insert the threaded needle through the hole at the top edge of the card on the inside and bring it up on the outside of the card. Unthread the needle, then return to the inside of the card. Rethread the needle and bring it up through the hole closest to the bottom edge and out on the front side.

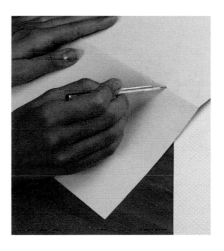

3 Turn the card over and Tie the ribbon in a bow along the spine of the card. Trim off any excess.

setting eyelets

Eyelets are beautiful embellishments and can be functional, too, as they can be used to affix other decorative elements to your hand-crafted cards. See page 11 for step-by-step instructions on setting eyelets.

Collage & Assemblage

One of the hottest trends in card making is collage and assemblage— layering and affixing random objects to make your cards a true piece of artwork.

To make a collaged card, assemble the items you are interested in using on your cards, such as bits of paper, pieces of vellum, fabric, beads, wire mesh, natural objects, even hardware! Play with the elements until you find an arrangement that suits you. Adhere the elements on the bottom layer first and continue adding materials until you're happy with the effect. Choose the adhesive that best suits the pieces you are adding to the card and allow each layer to dry before you add the next element.

Layered Vellum Card

Combine two hot trends—layering and eyelets—to make these oh-so-contemporary cards. The possibilities are limitless with the array of papers and eyelets available today.

materials

Metallic card stock

Blue card stock

Translucent vellum

Blue vellum

Ruler and pencil

Awl

Thin blue craft thread, measuring 6 inches (15 cm) long

Craft needle

Cutting mat or stack of magazines

Metal eyelet shapes

Blue metal eyelets

Eyelet punch

Eyelet setting tool

Hammer

step by step

1 Cut the metallic card stock to 6 x 8¾ inches (15 x 22 cm), the blue card stock and clear vellum to 5¾ x 8½ inches (14.5 x 21.5 cm), and the blue vellum to 2¼ x 4¾ inches (5.5 x 12 cm).

2 Fold each piece of paper in half, matching the corners exactly. Hold the edges together with one hand and press down along the crease with a bone folder.

3 Stack the folded sheets together, one inside the next, with the metallic paper on the outside, then the vellum, and the blue paper on the inside. Open the stack of paper and place the folded edge down. With a pencil, lightly mark the center point of the fold, then mark ¾ inch (2 cm) away from the center point on each side.

4 Holding all the layers together, carefully poke through each pencil mark with the awl. Be sure to go through all three sheets of paper.

5 To add the thread, start sewing from the inside of the card. Bring the needle up through the center hole, leaving a tail of thread long enough to tie a knot later. Sew down through the top hole, then back up through the bottom hole, and down again through the center hole where you started. Knot the thread, and cut off the excess. (Note: If you'd rather use ribbon instead, you may need to poke the ribbon through the hole with the awl. Don't worry about fraying the

edges of the ribbon, as you can trim them later.)

6 To embellish the front, place the piece of blue vellum on the center of the card. Secure the sides with transparent tape. (You will remove the tape at a later stage.)

7 Measure and mark 1 to 1½ inches (2.5 to 4 cm) in from each side. Open the card and place on a suitable surface to punch the eyelets. (If you don't have a cutting mat, a small stack of magazines will do.) Use the eyelet punch to punch a hole in the card directly over each pencil mark. Place a metal flower shape over the hole, and slip an eyelet over the shape and through the hole. Carefully turn the project over, keeping the eyelet in place. Set the eyelet as described on page 11.

8 Repeat Step 6 to apply the remaining flower shape and eyelet. Remove the tape.

VARIATION: Use the techniques above to create a different look. Place a piece of pat-

Designer: Marie McConville

terned vellum, measuring 4 x
5¼ inches (10 x 13 cm), onto
the center of the card front. Tape
the sides down with transparent
tape as you did in Step 5. First,
add the eyelets at the corners.
(You can remove the tape after
these eyelets are in place.)

Mark the center point of the
card with a pencil and add the
flower shape here as in Step 6.
To finish this variation, add the
eyelets between the petals of
the flower shape.

Designer: Terry Taylor

Peekaboo Window Corrugated Card

This mixed-media card sends a warm message of friendship. The use of dimensional stickers adds an imaginative touch.

materials

Blank corrugated paper card

Decorative hole punch (medium circle)

Pencil

Decorative papers (one solid and one patterned)

Scissors

Sticker machine

Message ribbon

Craft knife

Double-sided tape

Glue (optional)

Dimensional paper stickers

tip

This message ribbon is available with a variety of phrases for all your card-making needs. If necessary, vary the spacing in Step 6 to accommodate the words on your ribbon.

step by step

1 Open the card and place it face down on your work surface. Slip the hole punch onto the front of the card to determine the placement of the line of holes. Make a mark on the card at the end of the punch.

2 Lightly sketch a line down the inside of the card to use as a guide for hole placement. Make four equally placed marks along this line.

3 Align the center of the punch with the marks you made in Step 2 as you punch the four holes.

4 Cut two pieces of solid paper just slightly smaller than one-half of the front of the card. Run the pieces through the sticker machine to apply adhesive.

5 Adhere one piece of solid paper to the left half of the inside of the card, where the greeting will be written.

6 Cut the ribbon into three 2-inch (5 cm) lengths. Use the craft knife to make two slits—slightly wider than the ribbon—on the front of the card, spaced about 1½ inches (4 cm) apart. Make additional slits for the remaining lengths of ribbon.

7 Slip the ribbon into the slits and smooth the ribbon.

8 Trim the second piece of plain paper to fit over the exposed ribbon ends on the inside of the card front. Adhere the paper.

9 Cut a piece of decorative paper about 1 x 4 inches (2.5 x 10 cm). Slip it behind the ribbon. Use a small piece of double-sided tape or glue to secure it.

10 Close the card and adhere the stickers to the inside of the card so they show through the holes in the front.

Tickled Pink Cards

Whether you send these cards for a simple greeting or a special occasion, the recipients will certainly be tickled pink. Color is the key to this project.

materials

Hot pink card stock

Vellum envelope

Pencil

Craft knife

Metal ruler

Patterned scrapbook paper

Double-sided tape or glue stick

Floral embellishments (such as crocheted, pressed, or vintage sequin flowers)

Metal-rimmed tag

Rub-on lettering

Eyelet punch

Eyelet setting tool

Hammer

Brads or eyelets

Bone folder (optional)

tip

Always insert the card with the embellished side facing the envelope flap. This method protects your embellishments and provides a smooth envelope front for the address or salutation.

step by step

1 Trim the card stock to create a card that fits the vellum envelope.

2 Mark a square on the inside front of the card. Cut out the marked square with a sharp craft knife. Use a metal ruler to keep your cut lines perfectly straight.

3 Mark a square of patterned paper approximately ½ inch (1.3 cm) larger than the cutout you made in the card.

4 Use double-sided tape or a glue stick to adhere the patterned paper to the inside of the card.

5 Decorate the patterned paper as desired, using the floral embellishments.

6 Use rub-on lettering to write a single word or phrase on the vellum sheet in the tag.

7 Use tiny brads or eyelets to attach the tag to the front of the card. (See page 11 for basic instructions.)

8 Fold the card in half, using a bone folder if desired.

Keepsake Cameo Cards

A vintage family photo is treated like a fine piece of jewelry in these heritage cards. Use decorative fibers and wire for a memorable greeting.

materials

Blank card, measuring 5 x 7 inches (13 x 18 cm)

Patterned scrapbooking paper, one piece measuring 4¼ x 6 inches (11 x 15 cm) and one piece measuring 1½ x 2⅓ inches (3.8 x 6 cm)

Clear-drying craft glue

Craft brush

Unpatterned scrapbooking paper, measuring 3¼ x 4 inches (8 x 10 cm)

Craft board or poster board, measuring 2¼ x 3 inches (6 x 8 cm)

Hot-glue gun and glue sticks

Decorative fiber in a coordinating color, measuring approximately 24 inches (61 cm)

Card stock, measuring 1¾ x 2¾ inches (4 x 7 cm)

Vintage photo

Metal-rimmed tag

Cutting mat or stack of magazines

Eyelet punch

Eyelet setting tools

Hammer

Scissors

Designer: Marie McConville

step by step

1 Brush a thin layer of glue along the back of the larger piece of patterned scrapbooking paper. Press it down onto the center of the front of the card, removing any air bubbles. Allow to dry.

2 Brush a thin layer of glue along the back of the unpatterned piece of scrapbooking paper. Press onto the front of the craft board, removing any air bubbles. Fold the paper edges over the board and glue down on the back. Allow to dry.

3 With a hot-glue gun, glue down the end of the decorative fiber onto the back side of the covered board. Wrap the fiber around the entire length of the board to form vertical or horizontal stripes. Glue down the remaining end onto the back. Cut off any excess.

4 Add hot glue to the back of the covered board, and then press down onto the center of the card.

5 Brush a thin layer of glue along the back side of the

tip *Worried about cutting up treasured photos? Just get a color copy made, enlarging or reducing your original photo's size if desired.*

Once you've made one heritage card, have fun making dozens of variations, changing the types of fibers and papers you use, as well as the papers.

smaller piece of patterned scrapbooking paper. Press down onto the small piece of card stock. Allow to dry.

6 Cut the photo to fit on the inside of the metal-rimmed tag. Use craft glue and a brush to adhere the photo to the center of the smaller piece of patterned scrapbooking paper.

7 Take the metal-rimmed tag and place it on the exact spot on the small patterned paper where you want it to appear. With the pencil, mark the spot through the holes at the top and the bottom. Place the paper on a suitable surface. (If you don't have a cutting mat, a small stack of magazines will do.) Punch a hole in the paper directly over the pencil mark. Take one of the posts that come with the tag and insert it into the top hole. Carefully turn the project over, keeping the post in place. Set the post as you would an eyelet (see page 11).

8 Repeat Step 7 to add the remaining post.

9 Add hot glue to the back of the card stock and carefully press it down on the front of the card.

Pop-Up Café Card

Your personal bistro awaits! There are so many fun ways to use stickers. This clever card is just one of them!

materials

5 x 7-inch (13 x 18 cm) blank card and envelope

Array of decorative papers

Scissors

Ruler

Pencil

Rubber cement

Card stock

Instant-bonding glue

Teapot and teacup stickers

Decorative-edged scissors

step by step

1 Select the decorative papers for the floor and wall of your pop-up café. Cut one 5- x 7-inch (13 x 18 cm) rectangle from each paper. Use rubber cement to glue the papers to the inside of the blank card.

2 To create the table, cut one 9½- x 4-inch (24 x 10 cm) rectangle from the card stock. Measure and mark four fold lines in the rectangle: the first 1½ inches (3.8 cm) from the end, the next 4½ inches (11 cm) from the end, the next 6 inches (15 cm) from the end, and the last 9 inches (23 cm) from the end. Use your ruler as a straightedge to create four crisp folds in the rectangle. Fold the rectangle into a box and secure by applying rubber

(continues on following page)

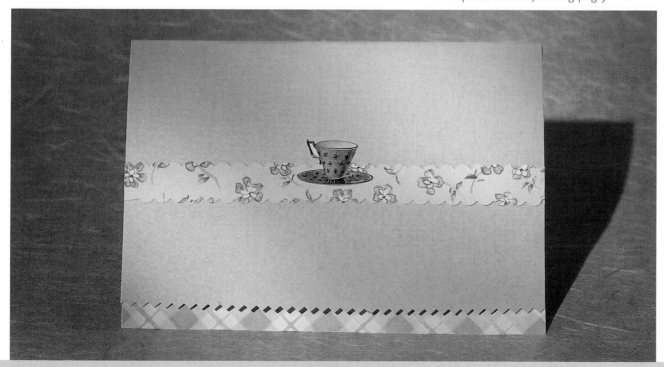

51

cement to the ½-inch (1.3 cm) overlapping end.

3 Select the decorative paper for the table covering. Cut a 4- x 4½-inch (10 x 11 cm) rectangle from the paper. Measure and mark a fold line that is 1½ inches from the end. Use your ruler as a straight-edge to create a crisp fold.

4 Flatten the box you made from card stock with the overlapped edge facing down, and use rubber cement to glue the decorative paper rectangle to the two exposed sides of the box, being careful to align the folds. After it's dry, glue the uncovered sides of the box to the bottom and back of the card.

5 Place the teapot and teacup stickers on a sheet of card stock, leaving at least a 1-inch (2.5 cm) border around each sticker. Trim away the card stock, but leave a ¼-inch (6 mm) tab of card stock at the bottom of each sticker. Fold the tabs at a right angle so the teapot and teacup stand upright.

6 Apply the instant-bonding glue to the strip extending from the bottom of the teapot and attach it to the table, 1 inch from the back of the card. Apply instant-bonding glue to the teacup and attach it to the paper table 1½ inches from the back of the card.

7 Cut a 1- x 4-inch (2.5 x 10 cm) rectangle from both the card stock and from the sheet of decorative paper you used for the table covering. Use rubber cement to affix the decorative paper to the card stock.

8 Cut out two ¼- x 4-inch (6 mm x 10 cm) strips from the rectangle you made in Step 7. Make a fold roughly ¼ inch from the end of each strip. Flatten the teacup and the teapot onto the table, face-down. Use instant-bonding glue to affix a folded end of one of the narrow strips to the back of each sticker. Make sure the side covered with decorative paper is facing up.

9 Create another fold in the strip that is attached to the teapot 1 inch from the point of attachment. Create a fold in the strip that is attached

to the teacup 1½ inches from the point of attachment. Trim each strip, leaving a tab that is roughly ¼ inch from the final fold. Use instant-bonding glue to attach each tab to the back of the card. (Make sure you are able to flatten the card after you attach the tabs.)

10 Trim the top of the card with the decorative-edged scissors.

11 Use the decorative-edged scissors to cut a strip for the front of the card. Use rubber cement to attach the strip to the card. Place a teacup sticker in the center of the card, on top of the decorative strip.

Designer: Megan Kirby

Personalized Cards

Assembled like small journals but designed to be given as greeting cards, these fun projects are a great way to showcase novelty papers, and can be made in any size or shape.

The surface of this card was embellished by sewing on sequins and seed beads.

materials

2 patterns of decorative paper

Sheet of card stock

Vellum

Rubber cement

Bone folder

Ribbon

Decorative-edged scissors

Straightedge

Eyelets

Eyelet setting tools

Quote book

step by step

1 Cut three 8- x 5½-inch (20 x 14 cm) rectangles, one from each of your decorative papers and one from the card stock.

2 Use rubber cement to glue the decorative paper to the front and back of the card stock. Smooth out any wrinkles or air pockets with the bone folder, starting in the middle of the paper and moving outward. Allow the rubber cement to completely dry.

3 Cut the vellum to a 7- x 5½-inch (17.5 x 14 cm) rectangle. Fold it in half and smooth with the bone folder.

4 Fold the decorative paper in half and smooth with the bone folder. Trim the side edges with the patterned scissors, then insert the folded vellum from Step 3 inside the card.

5 Make holes ½-inch (1.25 cm) from the edge of the top and bottom of the card, going through the front and back of the card and through the vellum. Insert the eyelets on the front side of the card and set them. (See page 11 for basic instructions.)

6 Thread a piece of ribbon through the eyelet holes and tie in a bow. Fold the ribbon over the top edge of the card.

7 Select a quote from the quote book. Trim it to fit on the second sheet of vellum, then secure in place with rubber cement.

t beautiful th...

in the world

...nnot be seen o...

even touched...

Designer: Megan Kirby

Vellum quote books are a popular item in craft stores, but if you can't find just the right quote, just type up your chosen message on your home computer and print it out on a sheet of vellum.

Best Wishes

Wedding Cake Card

Double-sided adhesive foam dots may well be a card crafter's best friend, letting you create three-dimensional effects from everyday materials.

materials

Patterned scrapbooking paper

Blank card or card stock

Contrasting card stock

Ruler

Craft glue

Adhesive foam dots

Cake stickers

Ivory satin ribbon

Scissors

Adhesive photo frame corners

"Best Wishes" vellum slogan or vellum and metallic pen

Designer: Beth Berutich

step by step

1 Trim the scrapbooking paper to fit on the front side of your card with a ¼-inch (6 mm) border.

2 Cut out a piece of the contrasting card stock large enough for your cake sticker to rest on, and glue it to the center of the scrapbooking paper.

3 Apply adhesive foam dots to the back side of the cake stickers, and arrange on top of the contrasting card stock.

4 Cut out a ¼-inch strip of background card stock and glue it about an inch (2.5 cm) up from the bottom of the card. Position your "Best Wishes" slogan on top of the card stock strip and glue in place.

5 Tie a 12-inch (30 cm) length of ribbon into a bow. Glue the center back of the bow to the top of the card. Arrange the bow's tails down each side of the card. Trim the ends in points and glue in place at their tips.

6 Mount your decorated scrappaper card on the front side of your card with photo frame corners.

Ribbon Closure Card

This popular card design, known as a gate fold, offers dozens of design opportunities. The ribbon closure creates a gift-like effect, inviting the card's recipient to "unwrap" their card.

materials

Sheet of card stock in a solid color

Metallic decorative paper

Dark patterned scrapbook paper

Light green patterned scrapbook paper

Light-colored ribbon

Clear-drying craft glue

Craft brush

Scissors

Craft knife

Pencil

Bone folder

step by step

1 Cut the card stock into a 6- x 11-inch (15 x 28 cm) rectangle. Cut the metallic paper to 4¾ x 5 inches (12 x 13 cm). Cut the dark patterned scrapbook paper to 4½ x 4¾ inches (11.5 x 12 cm). Cut the light patterned scrapbook paper to a 2½-inch (6 cm) square. Cut the ribbon into two 12½-inch (32 cm) lengths.

2 Lay the card stock horizontally on your work surface. Measure 2¾ inches (7 cm) in from each side and mark with a pencil. Using a ruler, score a vertical line along the marked spot on each side, creating a fold line.

3 Fold the flaps inward, creating a card form. Press firmly along the fold line with a bone folder.

4 Mark the midpoint of one of the long sides of the metallic paper.

5 Brush a very thin layer of glue along the last inch (2.5 cm) of one of the ribbons and press the glued end to the midpoint you marked in Step 4. Press along the ribbon's edge, then repeat with the other ribbon at the midpoint of the opposite side.

6 Brush a thin layer of glue along the back side of the metallic paper. Press down onto the center of the front of the card, taking care to pull each ribbon to the right and left side of the card front. Allow to dry. (Note: You will be covering over the card opening in this step; it will be reopened at a later stage.)

7 Brush a thin layer of glue along the back side of the large sheet of patterned scrapbooking paper. Press down onto the center of the metallic paper, removing any air bubbles. Allow to dry.

Designer: Marie McConville

8 Brush a thin layer of glue along the back side of the remaining sheet of patterned scrapbooking paper. Press down onto the center of the front of the card, removing any air bubbles. Allow to dry.

9 Slip a piece of thick cardboard or cutting surface inside the card, then use a sharp craft knife along the edge of a ruler to carefully cut a vertical line through the decorative paper that lines up with the card opening.

Pennant Birthday Card

Celebrate the birthdays of the special children in your life with pennant cards personalized with their photo and age. A collection of pennants looks great displayed across a wall in their bedroom, or pennant cards can be incorporated into scrapbooking pages.

materials

I sheet each of white and a solid color medium-weight paper

Clear-drying craft glue

White eyelets

Eyelet-setting tools

Photograph

Decorative-edged scissors

Photo tabs

Embroidered letter

Two pieces of scrap paper, one a light color and one dark

Piercing tool

Ribbons

Happy Birthday stamp

Embossing powder and gun

Flower-shaped brads

step by step

1 Cut a triangle from the solid color of paper, referring to the photo as a guide.

2 Cut two strips from the white paper, one ¾ inches wide (18 mm) and the length of your triangle's largest side and a second ¼ inch wide (6 mm) and 8 inches (20 cm) long.

3 Glue the ¾-inch white border strip to the edge of the triangle, trimming the sides to match the shape of the pennant.

4 Trim the ¼-inch border strip into four 2-inch (5 cm) lengths. Position two of the

lengths at the top and two at the bottom, then secure them in place with eyelets.

5 Trim the birthday boy or girl's photo to match the angle of the pennant, then cut a background that's slightly larger from the white paper with the decorative-edged scissors. Attach the photo with mounting tabs, then attach the framed photo to the pennant. Remove the adhesive backing from the embroidered letter and position it next to the photo.

6 To make the tag, cut a 2- x 4-inch rectangle from your darker scrap paper. Add an eyelet to the center top.

Designer: Suzie Millions

7 Cut a 1- x 2-inch rectangle from your pennant paper and glue it to the bottom of the tag.

8 Cut narrow strips of varying lengths from your light scrap paper to serve as flower stems, and glue them onto the tag, referring to the photo as a guide.

9 Make small holes in the tag just above each stem and insert a flower brad, then cut a wavy strip of white paper, and glue it at the base of the stems.

10 Stamp and emboss Happy Birthday at the bottom of the tag, then secure the tag to the pennant by tying ribbon through the eyelets.

Christmas Tree Card

Short of opening presents, decorating the Christmas tree may be the most beloved tradition of the holiday season. Miniature Christmas bulbs and colored glass beads let you have the same fun "decorating" a tree on the front of a card.

materials

- 1 sheet each of red, green, and brown card stock
- Scissors
- Ruler and pencil
- Decorative-edged scissors
- Glue stick or craft glue
- Awl
- Rubber hammer
- Wooden or plastic cutting board
- Miniature Christmas bulbs or beads
- Metallic gold embroidery thread
- Embroidery needle

step by step

1 Cut a 7- x 10-inch (18 x 25 cm) rectangle from the red paper. Fold the paper in half lengthwise to form the card.

2 Cut a tree shape from the green paper with decorative-edged scissors by cutting a triangle shape on the paper's fold. You may wish to experiment to try creating more interesting tree shapes by folding the paper in half and cutting a triangle. Cut a trunk from the brown paper using regular scissors.

3 Glue the tree and trunk to the front of the card.

4 Lay the card out flat on the cutting board and mark the areas where you wish to add miniature Christmas bulbs or beads with light pencil marks. Make a mark for the star at the top of the tree as well.

5 Use the awl and hammer to punch two holes — one $1/16$ inch (1.5 mm) and the other $1/16$ inch below — each of the pencil marks.

6 Attach the bulbs or beads with the metallic thread, coming up from the bottom of the card in the bottom hole, threading the bulb or bead on the embroidery needle, and then going back down the through the top hole. Tie off any thread ends on the back side of the card.

7 To make the star, wrap metallic thread once around two fingers. Remove the loop from your fingers, then tie a piece of thread around the center of the loop. Tie a knot in the thread and trim the edges, referring to the photo as a guide. Sew the star onto the card as you did the bulbs or beads.

8 With the decorative-edged scissors, cut a piece of green paper large enough to cover the thread knots on the inside of the card and glue it in place.

Designer: Megan Kirby

Designer: Megan Kirby

Gingerbread Men Christmas Card

Spread a little Christmas cheer — and have a great time crafting — with this festive holiday card. You can purchase the gingerbread men, or make them yourself with polymer clay.

materials

1 sheet each of green, white, and brown card stock

Scissors

Bone folder

Ruler and pencil

Decorative-edged scissors

Clear-drying craft glue

Hot-glue gun and glue sticks

2 small gingerbread men

White puff paint

step by step

1 Cut a 7- x 10-inch (18 x 25 cm) rectangle from the green paper. Fold the paper in half lengthwise, then smooth with a bone folder.

2 Cut a base for the house to rest on from the white paper about 2 inches (5 cm) high and the width of the card with a gentle arc in it.

3 Cut the house form from the brown paper and the snow-capped roof from the white paper using the decorative-edged scissors. Glue the house and snow to the front of the green card using craft glue or glue stick.

4 Attach the gingerbread men to the front of the card with the glue gun.

5 Decorate the background of the card with dots of white puff paint to create snow pattern on the front of the card.

tip *Transform the gingerbread house into a tree ornament by threading gold embroidery floss through the center top of the house.*

Heart Bouquet Card

What would Valentine's Day be without red roses and hearts? This card features both, with layers of vellum and decorative paper tied together with ribbon. If you're giving the card with a gift, make an extra rose or two for the gift tag.

materials

Red tissue paper

1 sheet each of red and light green card stock

Sheet of vellum

Sheet of lightweight, decorative paper

Scissors

Decorative-edged scissors

Ruler and pencil

Awl

Hammer (rubber)

Wooden or plastic cutting board

Narrow ribbon

Floral wire

Wire cutters

Floral tape

Glue gun and glue sticks

step by step

1 Cut three 8- x 2-inch (20 x 5 cm) rectangles of tissue paper. Stack the sheets and fold them in half lengthwise. Repeat twice more to create a total of three stacked sheets, one for each rose bud.

2 Create a rose bud by rolling one set of the stacked sheets into a small cylinder, angling the paper as you near the end to create the appearance of outer petals. Twist the end to secure.

3 Cut a 4-inch (10 cm) length of floral wire and lay it against the tissue paper bud. Secure the bottom of the bud and the wire together with floral tape, spiraling the tape down the wire at an angle and stretching it slightly as you work.

4 Use decorative-edged scissors to cut leaf shapes from the green paper, then attach the leaves to the rose stem by folding them around the wire and wrapping with floral tape.

5 Repeat Steps 2 through 4 to finish two more stemmed roses.

6 Fold the red card stock, the vellum, and the decorative paper in half lengthwise, then cut half a heart shape on the fold. Cut the vellum hearts with decorative-edged scissors, then cut out the red heart with plain scissors about 1/8 inch (3 mm) in from the edge.

7 Lay the three roses on the front of the card. If the stems extend over the edge, clip their ends with wire cutters. Create a bouquet by tying the roses together with a length of ribbon, wrapping the bouquet in a criss-cross pattern. Secure the ribbon ends in a knot positioned on the bouquet's back side and trim any excess ribbon.

8 Lay the card out flat on the cutting board. Make a pencil mark about 1/2 inch (1.25 cm) down from the top of the spine and 1 inch (2.5 cm) up from the bottom of the spine.

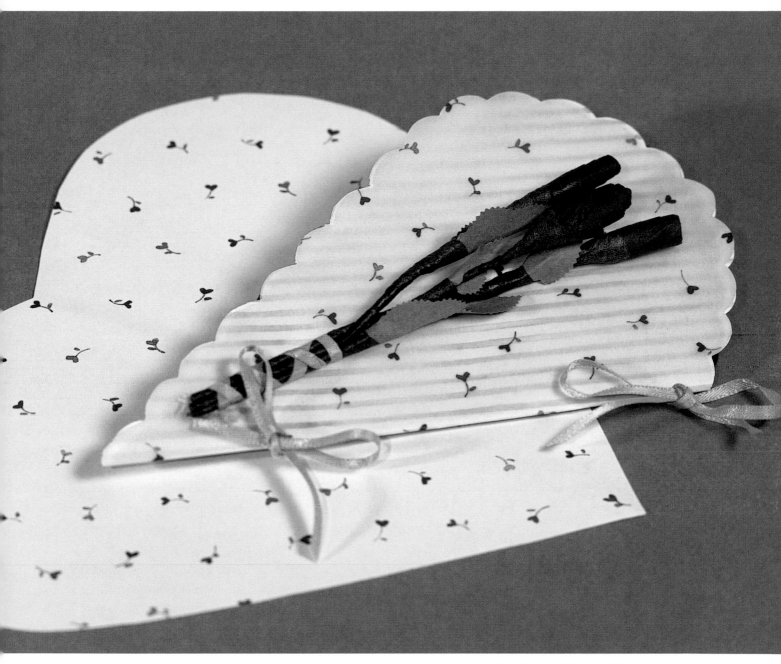

Designer: Megan Kirby

9 Use the awl and hammer to punch two holes — one 1/16 inch (1.5 mm) above and one 1/16 inch below each of the pencil marks.

10 Use the awl to force a length of ribbon through the holes from the back side so the ends are on the front side of the card. Tie the ribbons in bows.

11 Hot-glue the bouquet to the front of the card at an angle.

tip

Instead of hot-gluing the roses to the front of the card, attach them with the same tying technique described in Step 10. Be sure to add a note in the card letting the recipient know the bouquet can be untied and placed in a small vase.

Keepsake Invitation

Discover detail after exquisite detail in this handcrafted wedding invitation. Look for layered papers, embroidery, decorative shapes, and ribbon accents.

materials

3 sheets of printed ivory or white vellum, each a different pattern

Sheet of plain ivory vellum

Sheet of ivory card stock

Sheet of ivory corrugated cardboard

Heart brad

Narrow ribbon

Ruler and pencil

Scissors

Embroidery needle and white and green embroidery floss

Computer and printer

Decorative-edged scissors

Craft knife

Clear-drying craft glue

Paper piercing tool

step by step

1 Cut a 5- x 6½-inch (12.5 x 16.5 cm) rectangle from your ivory cardstock, then cut a 6½-inch square from one of your printed vellums.

2 Cut a 5- x ½-inch (12.5 x 1.25 cm) rectangle from another of your printed vellums. Add a decorative edge with your scissors to one of the long sides, then glue it to the top back side of the card stock, allowing about ¼ inch (6 mm) of the decorative edge to show.

3 Glue the 6½-inch vellum square you cut in Step 1 to the back side of the card stock. Carefully fold the excess width around the right front side of the card. Crease well, then secure in place with a small amount of glue in the center, top, and bottom areas.

4 Use your craft knife to cut out two small hearts. Position them on the bottom of the card so they overlap some of the vellum you attached in Step 3, then secure them in place with a dab of glue at their center top.

5 Make a daisy stitch at the center top of the hearts and a second one just below it. Fill the space in between the two stitches with French knots. (See pages xxx - xxx for paper embroidery instructions.)

6 Center a 7-inch (17.5 cm) length of narrow ribbon on the bottom of the card. Fold the excess ribbon around the edges to the back side and secure with glue on the back side. Center a 14-inch (35 cm) length of ribbon on the top back side of the card. Secure the ribbon in place on the back side with glue. After the glue dries, fold the ribbon ends around to the front side of the card and tie them in a bow. Trim off any excess ribbon, and add a dab of glue under the bow's knot.

7 Type your invitation text on your computer and print it out on your plain vellum. Trim the vellum to 3 inches wide x 4 inches (7.5 x 10 cm) high. (Note: If your invitation text won't fit in these dimensions, just add the amount of extra space needed to the dimensions in Step 8.)

8 Cut a 3¾- x 4¾-inch (9.5 x 12 cm) rectangle from the card stock, then cut a second one the same size from another of your printed vellums. Cut a decorative edge in the corrugated cardboard with your craft knife, referring to the photo as a guide. Trace your decorative edging onto

Mr. and Mrs. Jimmy Sweet
have the honour of announcing
the marriage of their daughter
Ivy Mae
to
Andrew Thomas Millon
on Saturday, the fifth of May
two thousand and five
Fairview, North Carolina

Designer: Suzie Millions

the vellum with a pencil, then cut it out.

9 Measure and mark a window in the cardboard and vellum from Step 8 measuring 2¾ inches wide x 3¾ inches (7 x 9.5 cm) high. Cut out the windows with a craft knife.

10 Center the corrugated frame over the invitation text and secure them togeth-er with glue. Place the printed vellum frame over the corrugated frame and secure in place with a heart-shaped brad. Position the framed text on the front side of the card, and secure it in place with glue at the corners.

11 Cut a 5- x ½-inch rec-tangle from the corru-gated cardboard, and create a decorative edge on one of the long sides with scissors or your craft knife, then glue it to the bottom back side of the card stock, allowing the decorative edge to show.

Card Making Gallery

Above: This window card was decorated by stamping and embossing with embossing powder.
Designer: Megan Kirby

Top: Customize a graduation card by spelling out the graduate's name and adding three-dimensional embellishments.
Designer: Terry Taylor

Right: Layers of cut and pieced paper plus floral embellishments create this simple, colorful card.
Designer: Beth Berutich

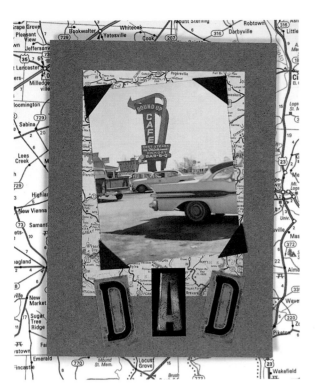

Above: An old map makes a great background choice in this handcrafted card. A family photo personalizes the card.
Designer: Terry Taylor

Top: Love pop-up cards but have trouble coming up with design ideas? Just wander through the sticker aisle at your favorite craft store for inspiration. The floral stickers in this card cried out for sunny skies and green grass.
Designer: Megan Kirby

Below: Illustrations from a high school science book were copied, dyed, and hand tinted, then mounted on a card.
Designer: Mardi Dover Letson

Above: A house-shaped button was sewn to the front of this handcrafted card, then stamped letters were mounted on backgrounds and glued in place to spell out New Home. Designer: Mardi Dover Letson

Book &
Journal Making

Journals and books provide a decorative framework for capturing and preserving the special moments in our lives. Fill them with photographs, sketches, doodles, quotes, signatures, goals, reflections, hopes, and dreams, then share them with people you love. The more fun you have creating and personalizing a journal or book, the more it will beckon you to fill its pages, and the more it will reward you through the years as a cherished keepsake.

materials

front & back cover paper

Ideally, a cover stock should be fairly heavy, but thinner papers can be layered on top of each other to create the necessary thickness.

text paper

Your journal's interior paper, or text paper, can be any medium-weight paper you like. If your book will include a lot of writing, choose a neu-tral-colored stock. Trim the edges of your interior paper with decorative-edged scissors or paper-punched patterns if desired.

ribbon & thread

Simple stitched bindings can be made with narrow ribbon, embroidery floss, and hemp. For books that will receive a lot of opening and closing, run your floss or hemp through a small pot of beeswax to strengthen the thread.

eyelets & brads

Eyelets and brads are a great alternative to stitched bindings, plus they add a decorative touch.

paper piercing tool

An awl, small hole punch, or other paper piercing tool is used to make binding holes in the cover and text pages.

bone folder

bone folders give your covers crisp folds.

basic techniques

simple stitching

Small pamphlets, booklets, and journals are easy to make with this technique.

1 Cut your cover paper into a long rectangle, then cut your text paper about ¼ inch (6 mm) smaller on all sides. Fold them in half and smooth with a bone folder, then open them up again.

2 Place your unfolded cover with its right side facing down on a flat surface, then place your unfolded text paper on top of it. Use a pencil to mark the spacing for stitching on the folded page stack. Here,

the simplest of pamphlet stitches is shown, which requires only three marks.

3 Use an awl or other sharp instrument to pierce through all of your paper layers in the areas you marked in Step 2.

4 Start your stitching at the center mark. To hide the knot, begin stitching from inside the fold. To expose your thread ends, stitch from the outside edge of the fold. Take the needle up to the top hole, put the needle through the hole, and then back to the cen-

ter mark. Put the needle back through the center and to the bottom hole. Run the needle through the hole, then back to the center.

5 Secure your stitched pages with a square knot. Trim the thread ends as desired.

6 If you don't want your stitched binding to be seen in the finished journal, prepare your cover and text pages as directed in Step 1. Place your cover aside, then stitch your text pages as directed in Steps 2 through 5.

7 Next, brush a thin line of glue down the fold of the cover, insert your text pages, and allow the glue to completely dry before handling the booklet.

no-sew book binding

Don't want to sew your books? No problem. Many decorative options await you.

1 To bind a book with brads, assemble your cover and text pages as described in Step 1, above, then use a holepunch to pierce through all layers. (Note: You can add designer touches to your binding by folding a narrow strip of colorful paper around the front and back sides of the folded cover, as shown here.) Insert colorful brads on the front side of the journal, then open them on the back side to secure.

2 Another option is to secure the text and cover layers together with decorative eyelets, then lace ribbon, yarn, or other decorative fibers through the eyelets.

Mémoires Scrapbook Cover

Like most scrapbookers, you probably invest incredible amounts of time and creativity in your scrapbooking pages. Why hide those beautiful pages under a plain cover? You probably already have the makings of a great cover in your supplies drawer.

materials

Blank scrapbook cover

Handmade paper

Scrapbook paper

Clear-drying craft glue

Bone folder

Waxed paper

Collage paper

Printed vellum

Printed tissue paper

Adhesive sticker machine

Press type or other
  lettering materials

Double-sided tape

Craft knife

Paper flowers

step by step

1 Cut a large square of scrapbook paper to place on your cover. Make the square as large as you desire. If your cover has a central opening, cut the center opening of your scrapbook paper slightly larger than the opening in the cover.

2 Tear several strips from the handmade paper, then adhere them with glue or acrylic medium to the back side of your large square so they peek out along the edges. Allow to completely dry.

3 Coat the back of the large square (which now has your handmade paper adhered to the back) with glue. Center the square on the cover, smoothing out any wrinkles or air bubbles with a bone folder. Cover the glued paper with waxed paper, then place a book or heavy object on top so it will dry flat. Allow to completely dry.

4 Cut strips and shapes of all of your papers—tissue, vellum, and collage—and set them aside. Tear additional strips so you have raw edges if desired.

5 Apply adhesive to the paper strips with the sticker machine, then play with position arrangement until you're happy with the look. Remove the sticker backing and attach to the cover.

6 Use lettering materials to add a title to your cover. In the project shown, the designer chose to add the French word "mémoires."

7 Add diamond shapes of vellum and tissue to the large square around the edges and over the lettering.

8 If your cover has a window opening, place an image, photograph, or even plain colored paper behind it, adhering it from the inside around the edges. A greeting card image was used in this project.

9 Glue paper flowers around the opening to finish the project. Voila!

Designer: Terry Taylor

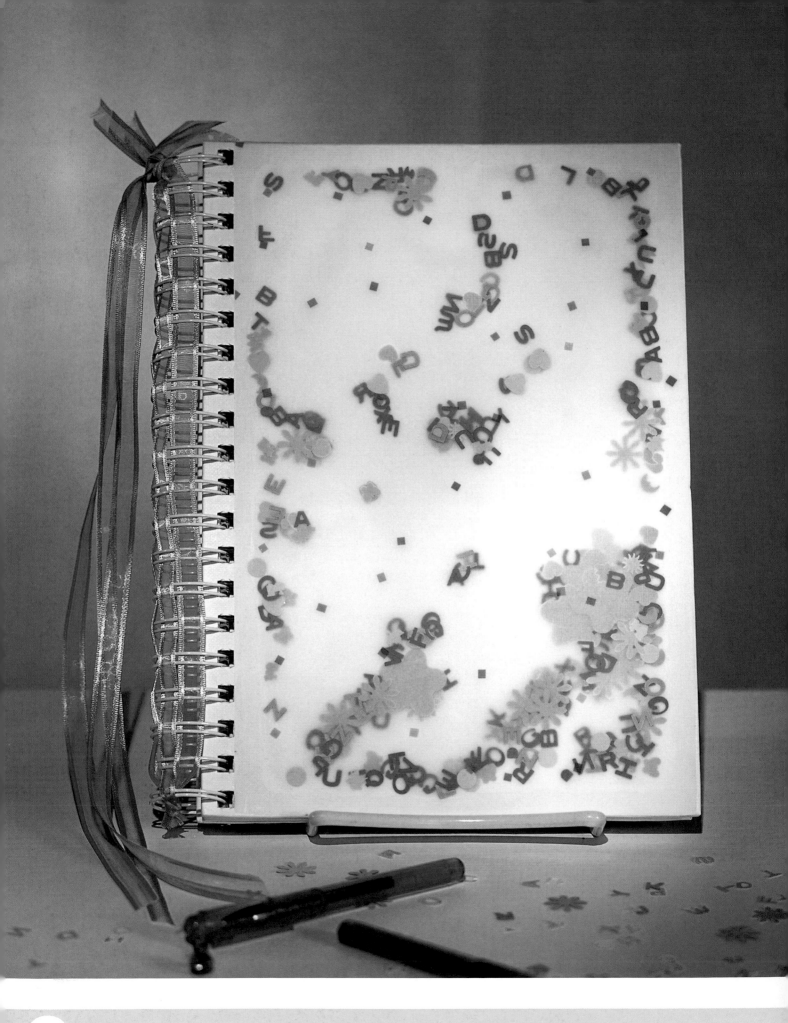

Confetti Journal

This simple journal can be made in minutes and makes a fun journal for grade-school kids. Change the colors and confetti shapes to suit your personality.

materials

Plain white journal

Ruler

Scissors

Sheet of vellum with confetti pattern

Paper punches of various shapes

Colored paper

Confetti letters

Confetti squares

Multipurpose, clear-drying glue

18-inch (46 cm) lengths of narrow ribbon in several colors

step by step

1 Measure and cut a sheet of vellum to size, using the journal cover as a template.

2 Squeeze a thin line of glue around both sides and the bottom edges of the journal. Press the vellum in place, creating a top pocket to insert the confetti.

3 Using paper punches of various sizes, punch shapes from the sheets of colored paper, then fill the pocket with your handmade and purchased confetti.

4 Squeeze a thin line of glue on the top edge and press closed.

5 Weave the colored ribbon in and out of the wire binding, then tie the ends and clip the ribbon to the desired length.

tip *The vellum "envelope" on the journal's front cover can also be personalized by adding photos of a favorite pet, your best friends, party shots, etc.*

Designer: Megan Kirby

Romance Journal

Looking for a simple, never-fail recipe for design success? Handmade papers, paper flowers, beads, and gorgeous ribbon are a winning combination every time.

materials

Journal making kit or blank journal

Handmade paper with flower petals pressed into it and assorted coordinating papers

Craft knife or scissors

Craft glue

Bone folder

Pencil

Ruler

Sheer ribbon, ¼ inch (6 mm) wide

Waxed paper

Paper flowers

Strand of pearl beads

Accent bead for ribbon marker

step by step

1 Begin by covering the outside of your journal with background paper. Cut the paper ½ inch (1.25 cm) bigger than the opened book and glue it to the cover. Use a bone folder to smooth out any wrinkles or air pockets, then glue the overlapping paper to the inside of the book.

2 Using the same paper, cut a piece about ⅛ inch (3 mm) smaller than the inside of the front cover, and glue it down, smoothing out any wrinkles or air pockets with the bone folder.

3 For the front of your journal, cut a piece of coordinating paper ¼ inch smaller than the cover. Center this piece on the cover and glue it down, again using the bone folder to smooth wrinkles and air pockets.

4 For the cover of the journal, carefully measure and cut the handmade paper ¼ inch smaller than the background paper. Glue the paper onto the center of the background paper, smoothing it with a bone folder to remove any bubbles or wrinkles.

5 Using the ¼-inch border as a guide, glue the ribbon vertically and horizontally across the front and inside front cover, referring to the photo as a guide.

6 Place a sheet of waxed paper on the inside front cover of your book and one on the outside of your journal. Stack several heavy books on top, and allow your book to completely dry.

7 Center and glue the paper flowers to the front of your journal. Glue on the pearl strand accents; allow this to dry.

8 If you are working from a journal making kit, tie the binding with raffia.

9 To create a marker, glue a strand of ribbon (longer than the journal's height) to the top inside of the journal's binding. Thread a bead onto the end of the ribbon and secure with a knot.

Designer: Diana Light

Garden Journal

Specialty books and journals are a great way to organize ideas, plans, keepsakes, and memories. The paper and embellishments are perfect for this garden journal, but you can easily create a different theme by changing materials.

White or ivory writing paper

Scissors

Bulldog clips or large paper clips

Paper punch

Heavy textured paper for cover

Decorative-edged scissors (optional)

Contrasing vellum

Card stock in solid color

Press type or other lettering

Hemp twine

Awl

3 small silver charms

A stick

step by step

1 Cut out about 20 4¼-inch (12 cm) square sheets of ivory or white paper for the pages for the inside of your book. If you've chosen handmade paper, tear the paper against a metal ruler to enhance the handmade effect.

2 Clip the pages of your journal together with bull-dog clips or large paper clips along the sides and bottom edge. Use a paper punch to make two holes for binding on the top sheet of paper about ½ inch (12 mm) down from the top and ½ inch over from the top side edges. Use the holes as templates for punching the remaining pages.

3 Cut the cover paper to a rectangle mesuring 10¼ x 5 inches (26 x 12.5 cm). Cut a decorative edge on one of the 5-inch ends if desired.

4 Fold the cover paper in half, then drape it over your writing paper. Using the inside pages as a guide, mark the area where the binding holes need to go. Remove the cover and punch the holes.

5 Cut the vellum to a 3½-x 5-inch (9 x 12.5 cm) rectangle and the card stock to a 5-inch square.

6 Fold the vellum in half to create a decorative top border for your journal. Fold it over the writing pages and make binding holes as you did in Step 4. Add a title to your cover with stickers or press type in the bottom center front of the vellum.

7 Position the solid card stock behind the writing paper, then arrange the cover and vellum in place so the holes in all layers align.

8 Cut three 20-inch (50 cm) strands of hemp twine and thread them through the right front of the book, through all the layers, across the back, and through to the left front side.

9 Place the stick in the front of the book and knot the twine strands around it on both sides in front of the hole punches. Secure the knots, then trim off any excess twine.

10 To place the charms on the front cover, use an awl or a craft knife to make three small, evenly spaced holes. Thread the charms on the twine and through the holes, knotting them on the back side. Trim off any excess twine.

Designer: Susan McBride

Boomerang Book

This miniature journal is perfect for collecting signatures, quotes, and special messages from friends. Each accordion pleat unfolds into a square page. After using, just let the pages collapse back on themselves and tie the front and back covers together with colorful ribbon.

Designer: Emily Greenelsh

materials

Scrapbooking papers

Cardboard or foam board

Scissors or paper cutter

Ruler and pencil

Bone folder

Clear-drying craft glue

Narrow ribbon

step by step

1 Cut six to 10 pieces of paper into 5-inch (12.5 cm) squares.

2 Fold each square on the diagonal, to form a triangle, then crease it with

the bone folder. Open up each triangle and fold the square back the opposite way, following the same diagonal fold. Again, crease the paper with the bone folder.

3 Open each triangle. Fold the paper in half, then in half again, creasing each fold with the bone folder.

4 Unfold the paper. Each sheet should have four squares, two with a diagonal crease.

5 Hold the paper so that the diagonal crease is parallel to you and two points of the paper are in your fingers. Bring the two diagonal folds together, carefully following the creases that have already been made in the paper. The two squares should collapse toward each other. Smooth the creases flat with the bone folder.

6 To attach the pages to each other, place one square in front of you in a diamond pattern, with the folded edges to your left. Place a small amount of glue on this square. Carefully position the next square—again in a diamond pattern, but with the folded edges to your right—directly on top of the first square. Smooth any wrinkles or air pockets with the bone folder.

7 Place a small amount of glue on this square, and position another square—with the folded edges to your left this time—into place and smooth it with the bone folder. Repeat Steps 6 and 7 for all the squares. Allow the glue to dry.

8 To create the front and back covers of your book cut two pieces of cardboard or foam board into 2½-inch (6.5 cm) squares. Cut two pieces of scrapbooking paper into 3-inch (7.5 cm) squares. Place a small amount of glue in the center of the squares, then center your cardboard or foam board into the squares. Glue the overlapping paper to the inside of the boards, folding the paper at the corners first. Use a bone folder to smooth out any wrinkles or air pockets. Allow the glue to dry.

9 Cut the ribbon into four 20-inch (50 cm) lengths. Glue about ½ inch (1.25 cm) of the ribbon to the inside face of the front and back covers. Place the ribbons on the center edge of the covers, on opposite sides. Allow the glue to dry.

10 To hide the seams on the inside of the covers, cut two pieces of scrapbooking paper into 2½-inch squares. Place a small amount of glue on the papers and position them over the inside seams of the covers, smoothing them with the bone folder. Allow the glue to dry.

11 Glue the front and back covers to the squares, making sure the ribbons on the bottom and top covers align.

12 Decorate the cover with layers of contrasting papers and/or with markers. This book's cover was embellished with vellums and scrapbooking paper layered in progressively smaller squares.

Embossed Heart Journal

How do you spot a true paper crafter? Walk through the premade journal aisle — where lots of quite functional but very plain journals can be found — and listen in amazement as they list off dozens of surface decoration ideas. The journal shown here was transformed with two layers of handmade papers, rub-on color, and an enamel-embossed heart.

materials

Corrugated cardboard

Black embossing ink

Scissors

Black embossing enamel

Melting pot or craft iron

Stamp

Embossing pad

Red glitter glue

Silver, gold, and red luster rub-ons

Black marker

Craft knife

2 sheets of contrasting decorative paper, one handmade and one embossed

Deckling ruler

Bone folder

Plain black journal

step by step

1 Cut a 2¼-inch (5.5 cm) square piece of cardboard for the base of the enamel heart.

2 Ink the square with black pigment ink or embossing ink and allow to completely dry.

3 Cover the square with a heavy layer of embossing enamel, referring to the manufacturer's instructions, then immediately cover with another layer before the first layer hardens. Add another layer or two until you have built up a heavy layer of melted embossing enamel.

4 Prepare your stamp by inking it with an embossing pad. As the last layer becomes liquid, place your stamp into the wet embossing enamel and leave it there until the surface hardens.

5 Gently remove the stamp and embellish the surface of your heart image with red glitter glue. Spreading the glue with your fingertips gives you more placement control.

6 Use silver and gold luster rub-ons to lightly antique the edges of the embellishment.

7 Trim the edges of the square with a craft knife or run them over a hot surface such as a melting pot or craft iron to remove any embossing enamel that may have oozed over the edge when you stamped the square. Color the sides of the cardboard with a black marker.

8 Tear a piece of handmade paper to a square or rectangle (depending on the shape of your purchased journal) slightly smaller than the journal's cover. Glue the paper in

Designer: Rhonda Black

place, then smooth with a bone folder. Allow the glue to completely dry.

9 Cut a piece of embossed paper slightly smaller than the handmade paper. Accent the embossed raised edges with gold and red luster rub-ons. Glue the paper on top of the handmade paper, then smooth with a bone folder. Allow the glue to completely dry.

10 Glue the embossed enamel heart and position it on your journal's cover. Allow the glue to completely dry. Enjoy!

tip *While you have your enameling and stamping supplies out, make a few extra embossed hearts, then use them to make a matching desk set, a refrigerator magnet, or even a brooch.*

Accordion Fold Book

The expanding pages of an accordion-style book are ideal for documenting change over time—a baby's first year or a house being built, for example.

materials

Illustration board

Several sheets of decorative paper

Heavy white paper for inside of book

Craft knife and box cutting knife

Ruler and pencil

Clear-drying craft glue

Photo mounting squares

Bone folder

Decorative-edged scissors

step by step

1 Cut two 7-inch (18 cm) squares of decorative paper and two 6-inch (15 cm) squares of illustration board for your book's front and back covers.

2 To make the back cover, measure and mark a border ½ inch (1.25 cm) in from each edge of the back side of a sheet of decorative paper. Apply glue on the inside of the marks, then center a piece of illustration board on the back side of the paper.

3 Turn the glued illustration board over, and smooth the paper with the bone folder, starting from the center and working out to the edges, removing any wrinkles or air pockets.

4 Turn the glued illustration board over again, and apply glue to the top right and left flaps. Tightly fold the flaps over the illustration board, and smooth with the bone folder.

5 Pull the top flap to 45-degree angle, and crease the fold with the bone folder. Repeat this process on the bottom corners. Apply glue to the top and bottom flaps, and fold them onto the illustration board. Allow the glue to completely dry.

6 To make the front cover, use a box cutter to cut a section out of the remaining piece of illustration board. The size of the window can vary, depending upon the size of the photo you wish to display in the window.

7 Trace the size of the window in the illustration board onto the back side of the remaining sheet of 7-inch-square decorative paper. Use the box cutter knife to make two diagonal cuts (creating four triangle flaps) through the center of the photo window marked on the decorative paper.

8 Glue the decorative paper onto the illustration board, aligning the photo windows. Smooth away any wrinkles as you did in Step 3. Fold the decorative paper flaps through the center and onto the back side of the illustration board. Allow the glue to completely dry.

9 Place the photo you wish to use for the front of your book behind the photo window, and glue it into place.

10 To create the back cover, cut another piece of illustration board, and cover it in the same manner as described in Steps 2 through 4.

11 Cut the paper into strips 5¾ inches (14 cm) high and as long as your

Designer: Tracy Hildebrand

paper's length allows. Glue several of these strips together, overlapping one strip on top of the other ¼ inch (6 mm) where the ends meet. The length of your strip will determine how many pages you have in your finished book.

12 Make a fold along the left edge of the heavy white paper, aligning the fold with the left edge of the paper on the board beneath. Crease with the bone folder. Next, make a fold along the right edge of the paper, again aligning the fold with the right edge of the

paper beneath, and crease using the bone folder. Continue folding paper in an alternating pattern until the end of the paper.

13 Position the remaining board next to the first board to use as a guide. Apply glue to the last page of folded paper. Center the paper and adhere it to the second board ⅛ inch (3 mm) from each side. Smooth the paper from the center and work to the edges. Align the boards on top of each other.

14 To create decorative backgrounds for your

photos, cut several 5¾-inch (14.5 cm) squares from the decorative paper. Glue the squares onto the white paper, smoothing the paper with the bone folder to remove any air pockets or wrinkles. Repeat to cover all of the pages on their front and back sides.

15 Use decorative-edged scissors to cut frames from the remaining pieces of decorative paper, then attach your photos to the frames and the frames to the pages.

NOTES Notebook

The clever outer cover of this notebook covers the interior sewn "binding" and provides a great surface for collage or other surface design.

materials

Sheet of card stock for cover

12 to 15 sheets of card stock in varying colors (about four times more sheets will be needed if you're using scraps)

Craft thread or embroidery floss and needle

Decorative letters

Collage paper

Clear-drying glue

Bone folder

Pencil and ruler

Awl or paper piercingtool

step by step

1 Cut a 5- x 9¼-inch (12.5 x 23 cm) rectangle for the cover, then cut about four dozen notepad sheets measuring 4¼ x 5 inches (11 x 12.5 cm) each.

2 Measure about ½ inch (12.5 mm) down from the top of a note page and mark that area with a light pencil mark. Measure in 1 inch (2.5 cm) from each side edge along that line, and mark with a dot. Poke through the two holes with the awl.

3 Use the marked page from Step 2 as a guide to make holes in the remaining note pages by placing it on top of another note sheet and marking through the holes with a pencil. Once all of the pages have been marked, poke through each hole with the awl. Set the pages aside.

4 Place the cover rectangle in front of you lengthwise, then measure and mark in 4⁵⁄₁₆ inch (11 cm) and 4¹⁵⁄₁₆ (12.5 cm) in from the left along the top and bottom edge. Place the ruler down along this mark and run the sharp edge of a bone folder along the paper. Repeat with the 4¹⁵⁄₁₆ line. Now press the paper down on itself along those lines to form the fold lines of the cover.

5 Place one of the text pages along the right side of the folded cover, taking care to align it properly. Mark through the holes onto the back cover with a pencil, then pierce through the holes with an awl.

6 To sew the text block onto the cover, simply thread the needle with an 8-inch (20 cm) length of thread and guide the needle through one of the holes on the back cover. Place the entire notepaper stack on top of the sheet positioned in Step 5 with the holes aligned and guide the needle through the same hole on the stack of notepaper. Pull the needle through the top of the notepaper, then guide it back down the text pages through the other hole. The needle should move through all the pages and out through the other hole in the back cover.

7 Turn the book over, and knot the loose ends of the thread tightly on the back cover.

8 Embellish the front cover as desired. This book used a vintage-look printed calendar and some wooden letter tiles that were simply glued in place.

Designer: Micah Pulleyn

Simple Pamphlet Stitch Booklets

These booklets are incredibly easy to create and can serve as a wonderful creative canvas to showcase decorative papers and a variety of embellishment techniques. Use them for everything from a quick gift, an elaborate greeting card, or a simple portable notepad to take on the go.

materials

Decorative paper for cover

3-10 text pages

Craft thread or embroidery floss and needle

Bone folder

Pencil and ruler

Awl or paper piercing tool

step by step

1 Measure and cut your decorative paper into a 4¼- x 8½-inch (10.75 x 21.5 cm) rectangle, then cut three to 10 rectangles from the text paper measuring 4⅛ x 8½ inches, and three to 10 text pages, measuring 4 x 7¾ inches (10 x 19.5 cm).

2 Fold the cover paper in half, forming a square. Mark ¼ inch (6 mm) in from each edge, then fold each of the text pages in half to form square-shaped pages. Slip each sheet inside another until all sheets nest together. Slip the text pages inside the cover.

3 Open the stack of paper with the folded edges facing down. Measure ¼ inch down from the top and bottom edge on the fold line and mark lightly with a pencil. Also mark the center location between those two points. There should be three points marked.

4 Place the paper on top of a towel or other protective surface. Holding all the layers together, carefully poke through each pencil mark with an awl. Be sure to go through all sheets of paper.

5 Begin sewing by passing a needle threaded with an 8-inch (20 cm) length of thread

Make a quick shower gift by decorating the book with a stamped image of a baby buggy.

Designer: Micah Pulleyn

from the outside to the inside through the center hole. Leave a short tail of thread long enough to knot later. Sew up to and out of the top hole, then down the outside fold and into the bottom hole. Sew back through the center hole. The thread should now be on the outside of the book cover. Tie the ends in a knot or bow, then trim off any excess thread.

6 Embellish the front cover with rubber stamps, simple embroidery, collage, or any other surface design technique of your choosing!

Fall-Away Spine, No-Sew Accordion Book

Here's a handsome book that goes together without thread or glue. You simply fold, wrap, and tuck colorful card stock to make each side of the book's study cover, then slip an accordion book into this cover and secure the whole thing with a detachable paper spine. The book can be taken apart and put back together again over and over.

materials

7 sheets of card stock in at least 3 colors

Text-weight paper (must be at least 50 inches wide and 4 inches high)

Ruler or straight edge

Bone folder (optional)

Craft knife or scissors

Cutting mat (if craft knife is used)

Pencil

Embellishments for cover

Adhesive (if required for embellishments)

step by step

1 Start by making one side of the cover. Each side is composed of three parts, all made from card stock: a inner rectangle to give the cover strength, a vertical wrapper that goes over the inner rectangle (ours is dark blue); and a hori-

zontal wrapper (light blue in our example) that goes over this. The first step is to measure and cut a piece of cardstock into a 6-inch-wide x 4-inch-high (13 x 10 cm) for the inner rectangle.

2 Next, to make a vertical wrapper, start by measuring and cutting a 4-inch-wide by 11-inch-high (10 x 28 cm) rectangle from a piece of colored card stock. Fold to create a horizontal crease across the middle of the paper. (Use a bone folder, if you have one, for extra-sharp creases.) Fold two more horizontal creases, one 1½ inches in down from the top and the other 1½ inches (3.8 cm) up from the bottom (see figure 2).

3 You should now have a rectangle with four sections: two outer sections that are each 6 inches wide x 1½ inches high and two inner sections that are each 6 inches wide by 4 inches high. Use the craft knife or scissors to cut each corner at a slant, as show in figure 2.

4 To make the outer, horizontal wrapper, start by measuring and cutting a 13-inch wide by 4-inch high (33 x 10 cm) rectangle from card-stock. Use a color that contrasts or coordinates with the color of the vertical wrapper.

5 Fold to create a vertical crease down the middle of the paper, dividing the paper into two 6½-inch wide

Designer: Micah Pulleyn

sections (see figure 3). Then fold again ½ inch (12 mm) in from each end to create two vertical creases on each end of the paper (see figure 3).

6 You should now have a rectangle with four sections: two outer sections that are each ½ inch wide and 4 inches high, and two inner sections that are each 6 inches high and 4 inches wide. Use the

craft knife or scissors to cut each corner at a slant, as shown in figure 3. Repeat steps 1 through 6 to make the three pieces for the second cover.

7 You put together each side of the cover as follows: Take each inner rectangle of card stock and wrap it with a vertical cover, as shown in figure 4. Then wrap each of these with a horizontal cover,

tucking the ½-inch tabs in between the vertical wrapper and the inner rectangle on each side (see figure 5).

8 To make the accordion pages for the book, measure and cut a 50-inch wide x 4-inch high (1.27 m x 10 cm) rectangle of paper. Fold it in half to create a vertical crease with 25 inches (63.5 cm) on each side. Now make accordion folds

(continues on following page)

in the paper to produce eight 6 x 4 inch rectangles with a 1-inch wide tab leftover on each end (see figure 6).

9 Place the two cover pieces side by side on the table so the open 4-inch high edges are aligned. To secure the accordion pages to the covers, tuck one tab from the "book" you just made into the slit between the wrappers and the inner rectangle at the front of one cover. Repeat with the other tab and the other cover. At this stage, your book can still fall apart easily, so close it carefully and set it aside.

10 To make the paper spine that holds the book together, measure and cut a 2½ inch wide x 4-inch high (6 x 10 cm) rectangle from cardstock in a color that contrasts or coordinates with your covers. Measure and mark a vertical line 1 inch in from each edge (see figure 7). Fold in at each of these lines. When you unfold you should have a spine made up of three sections: a ½-inch wide center with a 1-inch wide tab on each side (see figure 7).

11 To insert the spine into the book, slip

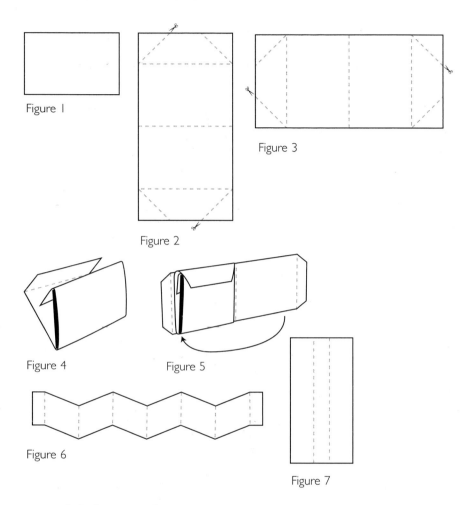

Figure 1

Figure 2

Figure 3

Figure 4

Figure 5

Figure 6

Figure 7

one tab in between the outmost piece of the cover and the inner rectangle on one side. Repeat this with the other tab on the other side. You now have an accordion book that will hold together without glue or thread, but can be taken apart to reveal all its various pieces.

12 Decorate the cover with stamps, cutouts, stickers, or scrapbooking embellishments as desired.

Ribbon-Laced Journal

For a completely different look, consider using colorful shoelaces, silk ribbon, or crewel embroidery floss to bind your books and journals.

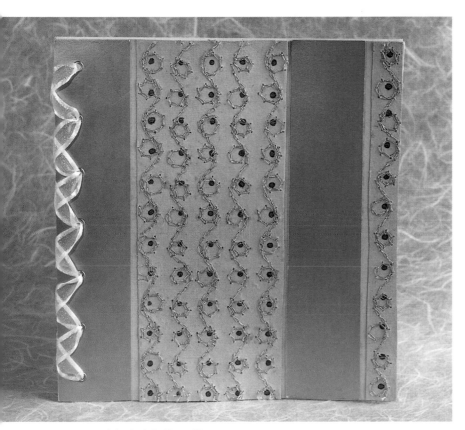

Designer: Marie McConville

materials

Card stock

Metallic paper

Decorative paper

Text paper

Scissors

Clear-drying craft glue

Bone folder

Metal eyelets

Eyelet setting tools

Hole punch

Ribbon

Embroidery needle

step by step

1 Cut the card stock into two 7-inch (17.5 cm) squares. Cut the metallic paper into two strips measuring 7 x 1½ inches (17.5 x 4 cm). Cut the decorative paper into two strips, one measuring 7 x 2¾ inches (17.5 x 7 cm) and the other 7 x ½ inches (17.5 x 1.25 cm).

2 Glue the metallic and decorative paper strips to one piece of your card stock, refer-ring to the photo as a guide. Use the bone folder to smooth out any wrinkles or air bubbles, starting in the center and work-ing out. Allow the glue to com-pletely dry.

3 Mark the locations with a pencil for 7 eyelets on the front left side of the journal cover, spacing them ½ inch away from the top and bottom edges and ½ inch in from the side edge. Set the eyelets on the front cover.

4 Trim a stack of text paper to 6¾ inches (17 cm) square, then align the stack under the front cover and mark light pencil marks on the paper through the eyelets. Remove the paper, and punch holes in your marked areas, then repeat the marking and punching process on the back cover.

5 Sandwich the text paper between the front and back covers. Thread the embroi-dery needle with the ribbon and lace the layers together. (See page 75 for more detailed instructions.) Tie off the ribbon on the back side of the journal.

Hinged Books

The hinges on these books are both decorative and functional, securing layers of writing paper between a front and back cover. Embellish the covers of your handmade books with collage, stamping, embossing, or anything else that calls to your creative muse.

3 sheets of 8½- x 11-inch metallic card stock, each a different color

5 8½- x 11-inch sheets white text paper

Decorative scrapbook paper, measuring at least 4 inches (10 cm) long

Scrap paper

2 decorative metal hinges with 4 metal brads

Scissors

Ruler

Awl

Craft knife

Stapler

Bone folder

Craft brush

Clear-drying craft glue

Decorative-edged scissors

step by step

1 Cut one sheet of the 8½- x 11-inch (21.5 x 28 cm) metallic card stock and the white text paper in half to form 8½- x 5½-inch (21.5 x 14 cm) pieces. Cut one of the remaining two sheets of metallic card-tock to 5½ x 2 inches (14 x 5 cm) and the remaining sheet to 5 x 4 inches (12.5 x 10 cm).

Cut the scrap paper to 4½ x 3½ inches (11 x 9 cm).

2 Line up the white text paper in a small stack. Take the narrow end, and staple through the pile in the center along the edge. Then staple once on each side. Set aside.

3 Mark the vertical center point 1 inch (2.5 cm) in from the edge of the 5½- x 2-inch metallic paper. With a ruler mark that center point all the way down the centerline. Fold the strip onto itself with the bone folder.

4 Bend each of the metal hinges around the folded edge of the metallic paper strip approximately 1½ inch (3.8 cm) in from each end. Once you have each hinge in place, use a pencil to mark through each hole on both the front and back of the folded strip. Set the hinges aside, then poke through each hole with an awl.

5 Place one hinge back onto the paper and insert the

metal brad through one of the holes. Carefully turn the paper over onto a protectve surface, leaving the brad in place. Set the end of the brad with an eyelet setting tool. Repeat with all the remaining brads and holes, both on the front and back of the paper strip. Set aside.

6 Measure 1 inch (2.5 cm) in from the narrow edge of each side of the larger metallic card stock sheet. Run the bone folder along that line to create the working hinge of the cover. Glue that 1-inch edge down onto the back and front of the stapled side of the text pages. Brush a layer of glue along the inside of the paper strip with the hinges, then place the paper around that glued edge of the book. Wrap the book in a sheet of wax paper, pressing between large books until dry.

7 To embellish the cover of the book, sketch a 4- x 3-inch (10 x 7.5 cm) rectangle onto the back side of the 5- x 4-inch piece of metal-

Designer: Marie McConville

lic card stock. Place the card stock onto a cutting surface, then cut out the rectangle with a craft knife to create the cover's frame.

8 Create a decorative edge along the long sides of your paper with decorative-edgeded scissors. Glue the decorative strips side by side onto the 4½ x 3½-inch piece of scrap paper. Trim off any excess paper.

9 Glue the collage block down onto the front cover of the book. Glue the back side of the decorative frame and press onto the collage block, pressing firmly along all edges.

Book Making & Journal Gallery

Above: The hexagonal shape of this drawing journal adds a fun twist to the traditional accordion-fold design.
Designer: Julia Monroe

Left: Handmade papers and a zigzag binding lend a distinctive air to this picture frame album.
Designer: Marie McConville

Above: The designer of this clever project raided her fruit bowl for inspiration and a base for a hinged, accordion-style book.
Designer: Julia Monroe

Below: The triangular shape of these accordion books creates interesting ways to divide up the page with alternating decorative papers.
Designer: Shereen LaPlantz

Above: A simple two-hole pamphlet design doesn't have to look plain — just have fun playing with differing tying and knotting options.
Designer: Shereen LaPlantz

Below: Tired of dog-eared, damaged journals that look like they've traveled more than you have? This simple travel journal was designed with a tube case, covered in a contrasting color of corrugated paper, that serves as a protective case.
Designer: Gwen Diehn

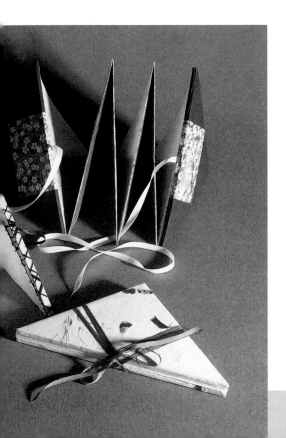

Decoupage

Our name for this centuries-old craft comes from the French word decouper, *to cut out. If you can cut, paste, and varnish, you can transform ordinary objects into sophisticated works of art. The technique couldn't be simpler, and you probably already own many of the tools and supplies needed.*

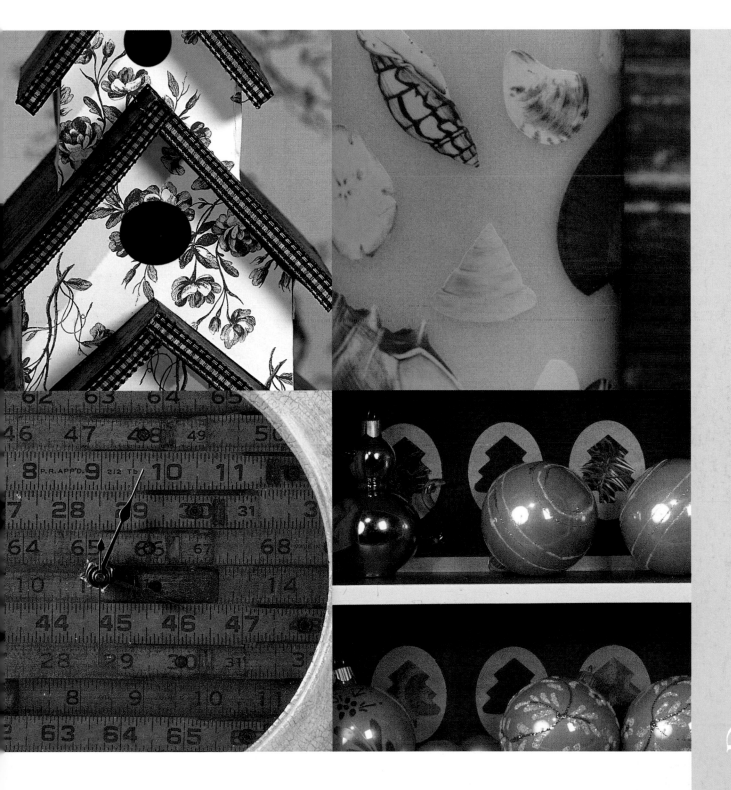

materials

cutouts

Magazines, gardening catalogs, gift wrap, sheet music, and even wallpaper can be used (in general, lighter weight paper works best). Remember you can make multiple copies of images, reduce or enlarge, and turn color images black-and-white with a trip to your local copy shop. Once you start collecting cutouts you'll find it hard to stop—dust-free plastic bags are a good place to store potential images.

Cleaning your Brushes

Very fragile papers may need to be sealed before you cut them out (if you cut first and then seal, the edges will curl). To use white glue as a sealer, dilute one part glue to two parts water, and swab this mixture onto the paper lightly with a soft brush. (Don't worry about small wrinkles that occur as the paper dries, they'll vanish when you apply the cutouts to your surface.) If you are using a commercial sealer, follow the manufacturer's directions, being careful to apply the product sparingly to avoid a cloudy effect.

scissors/craft knife

Sharp scissors are a decoupager's best friend. Use regular scissors to cut away large areas, small manicure or embroidery scissors when cutting small or intricate designs. A craft knife (with a sharp blade) comes in handy for cutting very straight lines and some detail work. Use a mat board or a piece of noncorrugated cardboard to protect your work surface when using a craft knife.

decoupage medium

This product is available at craft supply stores under several different brand names. It acts as an adhesive, sealer, and finish. Usually waterbased, decoupage medium cleans up with soap and water but leaves your surfaces water-resistant once dry (drying time is generally about 30 minutes). Most decoupage medium is available in matte or gloss finish, and new specialty versions such as a sparkle finish and an outdoor finish are also available.

adhesives

PVA (white) glue is usually a good choice for decoupage. Other options (depending on the material of both your cutout and the surface being decorated) include wallpaper paste, spray adhesive, and wood glue.

varnishes

Choose a varnish that suits the surface material being coated, and always follow the manufacturer's directions. Water-based varnishes provide a clear finish; oil-based ones will leave a yel-lowish finish. Along with matte, satin, and gloss finishes, varnishes are also available that impart colored, tinted, or crackled finishes. PVA glue can also act as a varnish.

paintbrushes

Use these to apply glue, paint, and varnish. Clean, high-quality brushes will provide the smoothest finish without leaving brush marks or stray bristles behind, but foam brushes are inexpensive and also work well. You'll want to purchase a variety of sizes and widths.

paint

Paint is sometimes used in decoupage projects—especially to cover the background of some surfaces. The type of paint used will depend on the object being painted.

paper sealer

If you're working with a thin paper whose edges want to curl, you may wish to use a paper sealer to treat your prints before cutting them. Sealing adds strength and durability to paper by adding a plastic-like coating, and it prevents paper from discoloring (and ink from bleeding) from contact with decoupage medium. You can make your own sealer from diluted white glue (it goes on cloudy but dries clear) or purchase sealer in craft stores:; print-fixative spray, shellac, and white French polish (also called "button polish") are just some of the products you can purchase to seal papers

basic techniques

preparing cutouts

You began your practice for decoupage back in kindergarten when you learned basic scissor skills.

1 If you are going to seal your images, do so before cutting them out. To begin cutting out, use regular scissors to eliminate excess paper by cutting a wide border around the desired image.

2 Use embroidery scissors or a sharp craft knife for the finer work. Cut exactly along the line using the entire cutting surface of the scissors, not just the tip. For the smoothest cuts with scissors, keep the hand holding the scis-

sors still while the hand holding the paper moves, gently feeding the paper into the scissors. Follow this same principle with a craft knife: move the paper rather than the knife, guiding the paper into the blade. Cut curves with the pointed edge of the blade; cut straight lines with the straight edge

3 Cut in one long continuous motion without stopping to get the cleanest cut possible. If white edges appear where you've cut, try cutting at a slight angle.

preparing surfaces

All manner of wood, cardboard, metal, and ceramic objects—practically anything with a hard surface—can be transformed with decoupage if prepared properly.

1 Use warm water and mild detergent to thoroughly clean the surface of the object to be decoupaged. Let the object dry completely. Sand wood surfaces. Use steel wool to remove rust from metal, then clean the surface with a solution of half vinegar and half water.

2 All porous objects need to be sealed with a sealant or varnish before being decoupaged. Prime wood objects to prepare them for painting. Wood objects you want to leave unpainted should be sealed. Metal sur-

basic techniques

faces should be primed with a suitable product; apply rust-proofing sealant for additional protection. Gesso can be painted on clean objects to create a smooth surface for decoupaging. Apply five thin coats in alternating directions following the manufacturer's directions.

3 If you want to paint the object before applying decoupage, paint several thin coats rather than a single thick one. Sand lightly between coats and then one final time with fine sandpaper after the last coat of paint so that cutouts will adhere easily.

applying cutouts to a surface

Once you've chosen and prepared your cutouts, all that's left is to artistically arrange them and apply them to your object.

1 Decide how you want to position your images on your surface. Play around a bit to find the most pleasing arrangement before securing anything permanently. It's especially important to plan ahead when figuring out how to fit images onto a curved surface.

2 Use a paintbrush to apply glue directly to the object's surface (not to the back of the paper or the paper may stretch and tear if you try to adjust it). Spray adhesive, on the other hand, can be sprayed directly onto the back of the cutout (just remember

to use newspaper or scrap paper to protect your work surface from the spray).

3 Using a clean, soft cloth, press the cutout down on the surface and rub firmly from the center to the outside of the image. Try to gently massage out any air bubbles—a sharp straight pin can be used to puncture stubborn air bubbles. Allow the adhesive to dry (follow the manufacturer's guidelines for drying time) and then wipe off any excess with a warm, wet cloth.

4 Apply a thin layer of decoupage medium or varnish over the images, following the manufacturer's directions. Make sure this coat has dried thoroughly before applying any more layers of decoupage medium or varnish. Additional finishes, such as

basic techniques

tint or crackle medium, should be applied last.

collecting images

Cutouts for decoupage are easy to find. Start off looking for simple prints without a lot of intricate details. You'll find these easiest to both cut and arrange. Gather more than you think you'll need—you may be surprised by the size of your images once you cut away the backgrounds. Collect favorite images from calendars, gift wrap, greeting cards, art and children's books, seed packets, and magazines. For the best results, use well-defined, beautifully colored prints on thin, but not too fragile, paper.

Test images with print on the back to be sure the back side won't show through when decoupaged. To do so, apply sealer to the front and let dry. Then, hold the image up to a light to see if the back shows through. If it does, you can try to gently erase as much of the print on the back as possible, or you can sand the back very lightly and then paint it with opaque white paint.

Avoid embossed or textured papers, very porous paper, magazine covers or other very glossy papers, foil paper, and prints that smear when sealed. If you want to use an image on problem paper, you can make colored copies at a copy shop, but be sure to seal any photocopies well with paper sealer because they have a tendency to bleed.

Save potential cutouts in large reclosable plastic bags; unused cuttings can be stored in the plastic pages of a photo album to keep them from curling.

Reducing the Thickness of Papers

Thick papers can be sometimes be difficult to use for decoupage, but it's possible to reduce the thickness of some papers and photographs by separating layers. Start by applying a thick coat of white glue to the back of the paper. Let the glue dry, then use a fingernail or the tip of a sharp craft knife to separate the paper's layers at one corner. Gently pull the corner toward an opposite corner to "peel" off the layer (or layers). Apply several coats of sealer to the front and back of the (now) thin image to strengthen it before cutting.

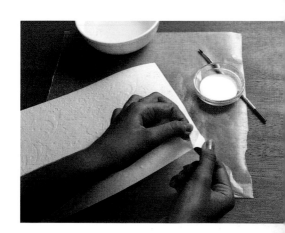

Toile Bird Tower

Is it possible to have too much toile? We don't think so! But even if you're not a toile lover, the wide variety of decorative papers available makes it easy for you to customize a birdhouse to match your home decor.

Tracing paper

Decorative paper with toile or other pattern

Acrylic paint for base coat (select a color similar to the background color of the decorative paper)

Black acrylic paint

Decoupage medium

Narrow decorative ribbon

Scissors or craft knife

Pencil

Paintbrushes

Sandpaper, fine grain (if needed)

Designer: Megan Kirby

step by step

1 Lightly sand the birdhouse, if needed, using fine-grain sandpaper.

2 Create a pattern for your birdhouse by laying the tracing paper over the front, back, and side faces of the structure and marking the face edges with a pencil. Use the scissors or craft knife to cut the pattern. Test for accuracy by laying the pattern pieces on the birdhouse. Trim if necessary.

3 Use these pattern pieces to cut out your decorative paper pieces. Set them aside.

4 Paint the birdhouse with one base coat. (If the color of the base coat matches the background color of the decorative paper, it will hide any imperfections in the fit of your paper pieces.) Allow to dry.

5 Paint the roofs, perch, and base with black acrylic paint. Allow to dry.

6 Use a small paintbrush to apply a thin coat of decoupage medium or varnish to the back of a decorative paper piece. Press the piece in place, using your finger to smooth out any air pockets. Continue with successive pieces until you have glued all of them in place. Allow to dry.

7 Apply a thin coat of the decoupage medium over the paper to protect from dirt and tearing. Allow to dry.

8 Cut a length of ribbon long enough to reach all the way around the edges of the top roof of the birdhouse. Lay the ribbon face down on your work surface and apply a thin coat of decoupage medium to its back. Starting at the front peak of the birdhouse, press the ribbon in place following the edges of the roof line. Trim any excess. Continue in this way until you have trimmed all the roofs. Allow to dry. Apply a thin coat of decoupage medium to the entire project.

Decoupaged Clock

The base for this clock is just a typical wood platter with a circular indention that's been given a special crackle finish. The clock movement and hands are available at craft supplies store. Add your favorite decorative paper for a one-of-a-kind timekeeper.

materials

Wooden platter

Clock movement and hands

Numerals (available at craft supply stores)

2 contrasting colors of acrylic paint

Crackle medium

Decoupage medium

Decorative paper

Scissors or craft knife

Paper punch

Small paintbrush

Drill and bit

Plate or compass

Spoon or bone folder

Designer: Terry Taylor

step by step

1 Mark the center of the wooden platter. Use a ⅜-inch (9 mm) drill bit to drill a hole at the center mark.

2 Paint the platter with two coats of the lighter color paint first. Let the paint dry completely.

3 Apply the crackle medium following the manufacturer's instructions.

4 Brush on a light coat of the darker color paint. Immediately wipe off the paint, revealing the crackled surface. Additional color may be added to intensify the crackles. Let this paint dry completely.

5 Measure the diameter of the circular depression in your platter. Then, use a plate or compass to draw a circle the same size as the depression on your decorative paper. Cut out the paper circle.

6 Use decoupage medium to adhere the paper circle to the platter, using the back of a spoon or a bone folder to press the paper firmly against the wood and eliminate air bubbles. Allow the decoupage medium to completely dry.

7 Create the borders that go behind the numerals with a decorative paper punch. Adhere these to the platter with decoupage medium. Burnish the borders with the spoon to eliminate bubbles or wrinkles.

8 Coat the entire clock with two or more finishing coats of decoupage medium.

9 Add the numerals and dots to the clock face.

10 Assemble the clock movement and hands following the manufacturer's instructions.

Flower Power Hurricane Shades

This easy, inexpensive project consists of simply decoupaging store-bought glass hurricane shades with tissue paper, but the results will shine! Choose colors and motifs to match your dinnerware, or go in a whole new direction.

materials

Glass hurricane shades

Tissue paper
  (four colors were used here)

Decoupage medium

Scissors

Decorative hole punches

Foam brush

tip *Punch a few extra blooms from your tissue for place setting cards or to decoupage the under side of a glass serving dish.*

step by step

1 Leave the tissue paper folded and cut it into strips of various widths.

2 Wrap a strip horizontally around one glass shade. Cut the strip to the correct length, allowing for a little over-lap, then cut the rest of the strips to this same length.

3 Brush a coat of decoupage medium onto the glass shade in a band approximately the width of one strip.

4 Carefully press the strip onto the shade, using the foam brush to smooth out any wrinkles.

5 Cover the shade with alternating colors and widths of strips. Allow the strips to dry completely.

6 Punch decorative shapes out of tissue paper. If you'd like to punch multiple shapes at the same time, fold a thin stack of tissue paper and back it with a sheet of regular paper to add stability, and punch on a sturdy surface.

7 Adhere the shapes to the shade in a random pattern with decoupage medium. Allow the tissue to dry.

8 Coat the entire shade with a coat of decoupage medium.

Designer: Terry Taylor

Out-of-This-World Photo Frame

Decoupage is a great way to commemorate any hobby. Whether you love astronomy, gardening, or travel, clip images from your favorite magazine to create a personalized frame.

materials

Wooden frame

Sandpaper

Latex primer

1-inch (2.5 cm) flat brush

Black and white acrylic paints

Pictures from magazines or themed scrapbook papers

Scissors

Decoupage medium

Clear acrylic sealant

tip

For a fun, splattered paint effect, load the brush with paint and hold it with the brush facing up near the area you want to splatter. Gently tap the brush handle with the handle of another brush.

step by step

1 Sand the frame well, then prepare the surface with a coat of primer. Allow to completely dry.

2 Paint the frame black and allow to completely dry.

3 Working outdoors or on a newspaper-protected surface, create faux stars by splattering white paint across the frame. (You may need to practice a few times to get just the right splattering effect — see tip below.) Allow the paint to completely dry.

4 Cut out and arrange your chosen images. Brush a layer of decoupage medium on the frame, then lay the pictures on top of the frame, gently smoothing out any wrinkles or air bubbles. Allow to completely dry.

5 Add a few larger dots to your frame by dipping the handle end of the brush in white paint. Allow to completely dry.

6 Brush a coat of decoupage medium over the entire frame. Allow to completely dry, then spray on a coat of clear acrylic sealant.

Designer: Diana Light

Beachcomber Candles

The decoupage images on these lovely pillars came from a sticker set, which makes the project super easy—no cutting required! Make several extra for simple, last-minute gift giving.

materials

Pillar and/or votive candles

Decoupage medium

Decorative stickers

Small paintbrush

step by step

1 Vellum stickers are great for decoupage. The see-through background allows you to use them on any surface. If you choose to use stickers with a color background, cut carefully along the inside border of the print. To cut smoothly, keep the hand holding the scissors still, and move the paper as you cut.

2 Apply the stickers to the candle, spacing them in a pleasing way. Smooth away any air pockets.

3 Use even up and down strokes to apply one coat of decoupage medium over the candle. Allow to dry.

tip *Napkins are another great source for images. Use them to decoupage candles that match your tablecloth and place settings.*

Designer: Megan Kirby

Faux Origami Basket

Have you fallen in love with the beautiful patterns of origami paper? So have we. And we've found that the paper is perfect for decoupage projects. Here's a beautiful origami basket with no folding required!

materials

Cardboard basket form
Selection of origami papers
Scissors or craft knife

Decoupage medium or varnish
Ruler
Paintbrush

step by step

1 Use the cardboard basket form as a template to cut appropriately sized sections of origami paper. (Since origami paper comes in standard size squares and your cardboard paper form may be an odd shape, you may need to piece sheets of the paper together to adequately cover your form.)

2 Cover the entire form with origami paper by brushing each piece of paper with a thin coat of decoupage medium or varnish and pressing into place. Allow to dry. Use the paintbrush to gently smooth out any wrinkles.

3 Apply one coat of decoupage medium or varnish over the papered form using even up and down strokes. Allow to dry.

4 You can stop here if you wish, or you can create greater durability and luminosity by applying additional thin coats of decoupage medium or varnish. Allow to dry completely between each coat.

Designer: Megan Kirby

119

Country Kitchen Decoupaged Cabinet

Use this simple decoupage technique to add color and flair to plain furniture. Roosters, fruits and vegetables, and flowers look great in the kitchen and can easily be added to other kitchen items to create matching accessories.

materials

Kitchen cabinet (or other flat surface)

Decoupage medium

Rooster prints

Embroidery scissors or other small, sharp scissors

Brush

step by step

1 Use embroidery scissors to cut out your rooster (or other image), holding the scissors still and moving the paper as you cut to avoid snags and sharp angles. If the background color of the rooster print matches your cabinet color, you can cut loosely around the selected image, leaving a thin border for contrast.

2 Lay the cut image on your protected work surface and brush with a light coat of decoupage glue/varnish. Carefully lift the image and apply it to the cabinet, gently smoothing away any air pockets or wrinkles. Apply additional images if desired and allow to completely dry.

3 Apply a coat of decoupage medium over the entire cabinet using even up and down strokes. Allow to dry completely before handling.

tip *Create a custom, antiqued look on your decoupaged furniture by aging the wood's surface before adding cutouts. The process is simple with the variety of water-based varnishes available today.*

Designer: Megan Kirby

Cigar Box Purse

Cigar box purses are all the rage, and they're easy to customize with your stickers, labels, and stamps. Check your clip-art collection for appropriately nostalgic images. You can purchase premade handles, or create your own with your favorite beads.

materials

Wood cigar box

Sandpaper

Clean cloth

Water-based wood stain

Metallic blue tissue paper

Craft glue

Decoupage medium

Labels and stickers

Craft paint in red, light blue, and gold

Rubber stamps and stamp pad

4 flat wooden beads

4 eyehooks

Round wooden beads, large enough for the hemp string and wire to fit through

Hemp string

Medium-gauge wire

Ruler

Scissors

Paintbrushes

Wire clippers

Needle-nose pliers

Designer: Megan Kirby

step by step

1 Start by preparing the cigar box. Sand it smooth and wipe it clean with a damp cloth, then apply the stain and let it dry.

2 To line the inside of the box, cut squares or rectangles of tissue paper slightly larger than the sides and bottom of the box.

3 Apply a thin, even coat of decoupage medium or glue to the inside of the box. Smooth the piece of paper for the bottom into place first, pressing the over-sized edges onto the adjoining sides to avoid gaps in the finished piece. Repeat with the side pieces. Brush a thin coat of decoupage medium over the paper to seal it.

4 When the decoupage medium is dry, paint and decorate the outside of the box as desired. On the purse shown, the top of the box is painted gold, the inside trim is red, and the outside trim is light blue.

5 If you're using stickers and labels, spend a few minutes determining their placement, then stick them in place. Apply a coat of decoupage medium to the entire box.

6 When the decoupage medium is dry, add any rubber stamp images. For instance, the purse in the photo has the number "25" at each corner. Apply another coat of decoupage medium to the box and let it dry.

7 To add "legs" to the bottom of the purse, simply glue a flat wooden bead in place at each corner, using the project photo as a guide.

8 You'll attach the beaded handles to the purse using two eyehooks per handle. Using the project photo as a guide for placement, insert the eyehooks.

(continues on following page)

9 To make the beaded handles for your purse, start by cutting two lengths of hemp string, each measuring 10½ inches (27 cm) longer than you'd like the finished handles to be. Next, cut two lengths of wire, each 6 inches (15 cm) longer than you'd like the finished handles to be.

10 For each handle, string round wooden beads onto one of the lengths of string, leaving a little more than 5 inches (13 cm) of string free at each end. Tie a knot close to the end bead on both sides to secure the beads. Don't trim the ends of the string yet; you'll need them in Step 12.

11 Thread a length of wire through each string of beads, allowing the wire to extend about 3 inches (7.5 cm) on either side.

12 Thread the wire and hemp at each end of the string through an eyehook. Fold the wire back through the last bead at each end of the string. Use needle-nose pliers to grab the wire ends and wrap them tightly to secure. Trim the excess wire with wire cutters. Tie several knots in the hemp string; then trim its ends. Apply a little dab of glue to the knots to secure them.

Decoupage a single image on the back side of the purse for contrast, or repeat the design you chose for the front side.

Decoupaged Holiday Curio Cabinet

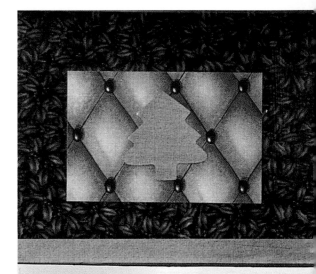

A variety of small wood cabinets are available (often found near framing supplies) that can easily be transformed into cherished showpieces with simple decoupage techniques. Cabinets for everyday use can also be made—the only hard part is choosing paper patterns!

materials

Wooden tabletop curio cabinet

Assorted scrapbook papers or holiday-themed papers of your choice (this project features nine different papers, six patterns and three solids)

Metal ruler

Paper cutter

Sharp craft knife

Small foam paintbrush

Decoupage medium

Large oval paper punch

Large Christmas tree paper punch

step by step

1 Choose different pairs of papers to use for each of the cabinet's outer shelves, one for the large background rectangle and one for the smaller rectangle. Choose the papers to use for the floors of the shelves, and the decorative elements, such as the ovals, trees, and molding strips.

2 Measure the height and width of the back of the curio cabinet's outer shelves, then use the paper cutter or a metal ruler and sharp craft knife to cut out the background paper for the outer levels of the

(continues on following page)

Designer: Marthe Le Van

curio cabinet. There will be a total of six rectangles, two of each paper pattern. For this cabinet, the background paper was cut into a rectangle that measured $3\frac{7}{8}$ x $4\frac{7}{8}$ inches (10 x 12 cm).

3 Cut out six rectangles small enough to allow a pleasing border of the background rectangle to show. For

this cabinet, the smaller rectangles measure 2 x 3 inches (2.5 x 7.5 cm).

4 Use the small foam brush to apply an even coat of decoupage medium to the back of one of the large paper rectangles cut in Step 2. Carefully adhere this paper to the back of one outer cabinet shelf, working from the inside corner and

smoothing out any air bubbles as you go. Repeat this process for each shelf on both sides of the cabinet. Allow the decoupage medium dry.

5 Use the small foam brush to apply an even coat of decoupage medium to the back of one of the small paper rectangles cut in Step 3. Carefully adhere this paper directly in the center of one outer cabinet

shelf, smoothing out any air bubbles as you go. Repeat this process for each shelf on both sides of the cabinet. Allow the decoupage medium dry.

6 Measure the back of the interior shelves of the curio cabinet. (In this example, the bottom two shelves were 8¾ x 4 inches [22 x 10 cm]. You may need to make a template for the top curved shelf.) Cut the paper to fit these shapes.

7 Use the small foam brush to apply an even coat of decoupage medium to the back of one piece of the paper cut in Step 6. Carefully adhere this paper to the back of one interior cabinet shelf, working from one corner and smoothing out any air bubbles as you go. Repeat this process for each shelf, and allow the decoupage medium dry.

8 Measure and cut the papers for the bottom "floor" of each cabinet shelf. There are nine pieces of paper in all. (Tip: You do not need to cut a curved angle for the front edge of the outer shelves prior to adhering the paper. It can be trimmed to fit later.) Carefully adhere the paper to the floors of the shelves with decoupage medium and let dry. Use a very sharp craft knife to trim the excess paper around the curved edge of the outer cabinet shelves as needed. For the best results, hold the knife at a 90-degree angle against the shelf as you cut the paper.

9 Use the large oval paper punch to cut nine ovals to decorate the interior cabinet shelves, and adhere three punched ovals to each interior shelf with decoupage medium. Make sure the paper ovals are centered, level, and evenly spaced. Let dry.

10 Use the large tree paper punch to cut 15 trees to decorate the cabinet shelves. Use decoupage medium to adhere one tree in the center of each small rectangle on all of the outer cabinet shelves and one paper tree in the center of each paper oval on the interior cabinet shelves. Allow the decoupage medium dry.

11 For the decorative molding, cut six strips of paper ⅜ inch (1 cm) wide by the width of the outer cabinet shelves. Cut three strips of paper ⅜ inch (1 cm) wide by the width of the interior cabinet shelves. Use decoupage medium to apply these strips to the lower edge of the back of each shelf, and let dry.

12 To finish the decorated cabinet, apply a thin topcoat of decoupage medium across all paper surfaces. Allow to completely dry before moving the cabinet.

Decoupage Gallery

Left: Room divider screens provide the perfect frame to showcase decorative papers. The paper shown here was created by pressing shapes of colorful tissue paper between wax paper with an iron on a medium-heat setting.
Designer: Terry Taylor

Right: Transform your Plain-Jane storage boxes into decorative home accents by decoupaging strips of bright tissue paper onto shoe boxes. Find a contrasting tag to add labels in the scrapbooking aisle.

Above left: Just when you thought you'd seen every possible decoupage surface, these eggs appear before your eyes! Patterns were cut from dinner napkins, then decoupaged to hollowed-out eggs.
Designer: Terry Taylor

Above: Vintage labels are one of the hottest new materials for crafters. For this project, a four-color fruit crate label (available in craft stores as clip art) was decoupaged to a large glass jar to make a cat food container.
Designer: Megan Kirby.

Above: Layers of decoupaged tissue paper cut in interesting shapes creates a translucent, designer effect on an inexpensive photo frame.
Designer: Terry Taylor

Right: Images from paper napkins were carefully cut out and decoupaged to candles.
Designer: Megan Kirby.

Paper Folding

Although many people associate folded paper crafts with traditional origami, the incredible array of novelty scrapbooking paper has opened up a world of possibilities for the contemporary paper crafter. Make a picture frame, a bouquet of paper flowers, or even a paper purse!

materials

paper

Look for papers that can hold a crease (see below.) Many specialty papers, such as vellums, are surprisingly easy to work with.

origami paper

Known for its traditional patterns and colors, origami paper holds creases well and is a good choice for beginning paper folders.

In traditional origami, square paper is the only material used. If you use genuine origami paper, it may be the only supply you'll need, since almost all origami projects begin with the basic square. Paper designed specifically for origami offers several advantages because it has the proper weight and grain for perfect folding.

If you're a beginner, you might practice with traditional origami paper so you understand how the paper should respond. But many types of paper can be used successfully in contemporary origami. Feel free to experiment. The most important consideration is that the paper you use folds crisply and repeatedly without stretching or tearing.

You can choose from traditional square origami paper, wrapping paper, handmade paper, decorative foil, even recycled magazine pages for a unique look.

cutting mat with grid

If you cut your own paper to size, a cutting mat with a grid is ideal.

bone folder

For many folded projects, the crisp edge created with a bone folder is a definite plus.

craft knife

A craft knife with a sharp blade will be handy for cutting paper to size.

metal straightedge

Use this indispensable tool while cutting paper and perhaps to mark your project.

pencil

Keep a pencil on hand for any marking that may be necessary.

glue

Depending upon your final project, clear-drying craft glue may be used to reinforce seams and folds.

scissors

If you find that you need a pair of scissors, the household variety will suffice.

Cutting Perfect Squares

If you cut your own paper for your origami projects, it's important to cut perfect squares so your folds will be accurate. There are several ways you can achieve the perfect square: use a small paper cutter; use a cutting mat with a grid and a sharp craft knife; or mark and measure your paper carefully and cut with scissors.

basic techniques

paper folding for general craft projects

Most papers can be successfully folded, although a few types produce poor results and should be avoided.

To test a paper's suitability for paper folding, fold a sample sheet in half, then run a bone folder over the fold. If the paper folds well and the crease is crisp, you've made a good choice. If the crease is thick, undefined, or fades away before your eyes, avoid that particular paper for folded paper projects.

paper folding for origami

Elegantly simple, or simply elegant? Both descriptions define origami, the ancient Japanese technique of folding paper. To begin, all you really need is a

sheet of paper! But the contemporary applications of the craft offer a variety of ways to express yourself and incorporate the fabulous papers available today. Learn just a few basic folds and you'll be ready to create works of art.

The essence of origami is careful and precise folding. Practice these basic folds to get a good foundation for more advanced crafting. Sharpen the creases by working on a hard surface and pressing firmly toward both ends from the center, or by holding the paper in the air and sliding toward the ends from the center. Since each fold builds on the previous one, make sure that each is done with care and attention.

Practice Makes Perfect!

Remember that even the most complicated origami project is simply a series of folds. Mastering the craft just takes a bit of practice. After a few projects, the folds will be second nature and you'll read the diagrams as easily as the morning paper.

origami: valley fold

To make a valley fold, place the right (or patterned) side) of the paper face-up. Fold the paper toward you at the indicated line and crease the fold.

origami: mountain fold

The opposite of the valley fold, the mountain fold is formed by folding the paper away from you, to the back of the indicated line. But you can also simply place the wrong side of the paper face up and make a valley fold as in Step 1—it's a bit easier than folding paper to the back.

origami: reverse fold

Reverse folds change the direction of the paper. To make an inside reverse fold, crease the paper to the front and then to the back, making the valley and mountain folds along the same line. Then open the paper and press along the folds to the inside of the paper.

origami: outside reverse fold

To make an outside reverse fold, crease the paper to the front and then to the back, making the valley and mountain folds along the same line. Then open the paper and press along the folds to the outside of the paper.

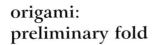

origami: crimp fold

The crimp fold incorporates two separate reverse folds to make a tuck in the paper, sometimes changing its angle. Make the valley fold and the mountain fold as indicated, open the paper, and fold along the creases. A pleat fold is created similarly, but the paper is not opened.

origami: preliminary fold

The preliminary fold is the base for many projects. Make it by valley-folding the paper vertically, horizontally, and diagonally. Pull two of the opposite corners together and fold them between the two remaining corners.

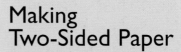

Making Two-Sided Paper

It's a lot of fun to make your own custom paper with two colored or patterned sides. Simply use a light layer of glue to adhere two different papers together for a personalized look; be sure to smooth the layers together.

Playful Party Hats

Pointy paper party hats aren't just for kids. Make your fete more fun with these easy toppers.

materials

Sheet of card stock per hat, measuring at least 12 x 12 inches (30.5 cm)

Hat and tassel templates (see pages 306 and 307)

Double-sided tape

Small pom-poms

Satin thread or very thin ribbon

Sheer flowers with wire edging

Ribbon or elastic cord

Photocopy machine

Pencil

Scissors

Glue gun and glue sticks or double-sided tape

Decorative paper punches

step by step

1 Make a photocopy of the hat template on page 306 and use it to cut out your paper.

2 Assemble the hat by rolling the paper into a cone and inserting the tab into the slot. Attach the flap to the side of the hat using either hot glue or double-sided tape. If you're using glue, allow it to dry before moving to the next step.

3 Now for the fun part: Decorating your hat! Use a hot-glue gun to attach embellishments such as satin thread, pom-poms, and pretty ribbon flowers. Some other decorative materials you might consider using include sequins, feathers, beads, lace, and anything else you can attach to your hat.

4 To create a snazzy tassel like the one topping the pale blue hat in the photo, start by photocopying the tassel template on page 307. Trace the template onto a piece of the same paper from which you made the hat and cut it out. Cut the fringe along the piece's edge, as indicated. Roll the piece into a cone, using a pencil as a guide.

5 Fit the end of the tassel that's not fringed onto the top of the hat and glue it into place. Then cut a ½- x 2-inch (1.3 x 5 cm) strip of paper in the same color and glue it over the bottom edge of the tassel on the hat to form a cuff. Curl the tassel's fringe around a pencil to finish the look.

6 To make sure your hat stays put, add a chin band made from ribbon or elastic cord: Use an awl to poke two holes directly opposite each other in the bottom edge of the hat. Then thread a length of ribbon or cord through the holes, securing each end with a bit of tape or a knot inside the hat.

Origami Photo Frame

Use this picture-perfect project to make the ideal frame for any photo, or choose coordinating colors to match the décor in your home. Once you master the folds, you can easily make a few dozen frames from your paper stash for last-minute gift giving.

materials

4 sheets of origami paper (or any paper that can hold a crease)

Bone folder

Glue stick

step by step

1 Cut the paper into squares approximately the size you'd like your finished frame to be.

2 Working on a flat surface, place the first piece of paper patterned side down in front of you. Fold it in half on the diagonal and crease it well using the bone folder.

3 Turn the triangle so that the long edge is parallel to your body. Fold up the corners on the right and the left to meet the top corner. The corner edges should meet in the center of the paper. (See figure 1.) Crease the folds well, using a bone folder.

4 Unfold the paper all the way and turn it so that the diagonal crease is parallel to your body. (See figure 2.) Fold the top and bottom corners into the center. (See figure 3.)

5 Fold the paper in half along the diagonal crease. (See figure 4.)

6 Fold down the points on the right and left so that their top edges meet the crease line. (See figures 5 and 6.)

7 Repeat Steps 2 through 6 for the remaining sheets of paper.

8 To assemble the frame, slide the point of one paper into the point of another. Place a small amount of glue in the folds to secure them together.

9 Slip your photo into the pouch in the sides of the frame.

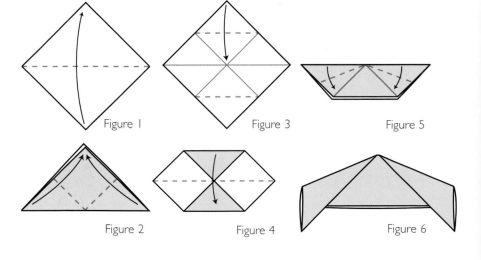

Figure 1

Figure 3

Figure 5

Figure 2

Figure 4

Figure 6

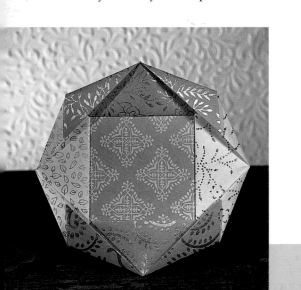

Designer: Rain Newcomb

Very Special Gift Bag

Whether it's a piece of precious jewelry or a really fine box of chocolates, your gift will be even more special presented in a stunning gift bag. Made from rich papers and elegant ribbons, this lovely bag could easily double as a party purse!

materials

Templates

2 sheets of heavyweight novelty paper, at least 12 inches square (30.5 cm)

Removable tape

Double-sided tape

Hot-glue gun and glue sticks

Wide wire-edged ribbon

Thin satin ribbon

Lightweight monogrammed pendant

Photocopier

Scissors

Self-healing cutting mat

Craft knife

Straightedge

Burnishing tool or bone folder

Paper punch

step by step

1 Photocopy and enlarge the templates on pages 300 through 302, then cut them out. Decide which paper you'd like for the side panels and which you'd like for the body of the bag.

2 Position your pattern pieces on the paper sheets, using bits of white artist's tape to hold the patterns in place. (The artist's tape will hold the paper secure without damaging it.)

3 Place the paper and patterns on a self-healing cutting mat. Cut out each piece with a sharp craft knife, using a straightedge to guide the blade and make accurate cuts.

4 With the pattern pieces still taped to the paper cutouts, fold the pieces, following the dotted lines on the patterns. To make sharp, crisp folds, run a bone folder along the folds. Remove the artist's tape and set aside the pattern pieces.

5 The side panels are attached to the body of the purse with double-sided tape right along the edges of the flaps you folded in Step 4. Before applying the tape, check its placement: Fit the side panels into the body and mark the outer edges where the tape will go. Then remove the panels and carefully apply the tape. Fit the side panels back in, one at a time, using gentle pressure to seal the pieces together.

6 Now, add embellishments to the bag. Cut two half-moons from a different color of paper, as wide from tip to tip as the top edge of the bag. Use double-sided tape to attach a half-moon to each face of the bag.

7 Cut a length of thin satin ribbon, thread it through the top of the monogrammed pendant, and tie it into a bow. Then attach the monogrammed pendant to the center of one of the half-moons with a bead of hot glue.

Designer: Susan McBride

8 Next, make the bag's ribbon handle. Determine
how long you'd like the handle
to be; then cut a length of wire-
edged ribbon a few inches
longer than that. Using the
project photo as a guide, punch
a hole in each side of the bag

and thread the ribbon through
these holes. Secure the ribbon
by tying a knot at each end on
the inside of the bag.

tip

*Almost everything in your
crafter's embellishment stash
can be used to decorate a gift
bag or purse. Paper flowers,
beads, stickers . . . you name it!*

Accordion Files

Keeping your work space neat and tidy is much easier when you have great-looking files where you can stash your stuff.

materials

2 sheets of heavyweight paper in contrasting colors

Twine, string, or a narrow ribbon for the tie

Double-sided tape

2 paper brads

Pencil

Ruler

Scissors

Bone folder

Decorative paper punch (optional)

Craft knife

step by step

1 Each file consists of a file body made from one color of paper, two accordion-folded sides made from paper in a contrasting color, and two fasteners.

2 Start by making the body of the folder. Cut a rectangle measuring 13 x 26 inches (33 x 66 cm) from one of the sheets of heavyweight paper. Save the scraps for the fasteners (see Step 9).

3 You'll make four parallel folds across the shorter width of the rectangle to create the two broad sides, the flat bottom, and the flap of the file body. To mark the position of these folds, measure in from the edge of one of the short sides and, using a pencil and ruler, strike a light line across the rec-

tangle at the following points: 9 inches (22 cm), 11 inches (28 cm), 18 inches (46 cm), and 20 inches (51 cm). This will leave 4 inches (10 cm) for the file flap.

4 Score the fold lines: Place the edge of the ruler along each marked line and score it by running your bone folder along the edge. Fold the rectangle at the scored lines to create the body of your file folder.

5 Next, make the accordion-folded sides. From the other sheet of heavyweight paper, measure and cut two 8-inch (20 cm) squares, saving the scraps to make the fasteners (see Step 9). Mark fold lines at $5/8$-inch (2 cm) intervals on both squares. You'll end up with 11 lines on each one, with the last line

marking off a shorter fold than the others. Use the bone folder and ruler to score the fold lines; then fan fold each square. Now, snip off each square's short fold with your scissors.

6 You'll attach the accordion-folded sides to the file body using the double-sided tape. Although you'll apply the tape to the accordion-folded side, when the side is in place, the tape should be positioned so that it runs along the edge (rather than the inside) of the file body. Before applying the tape to the sides, determine where to place it first. To do this, fit one of the accordion-folded sides into one side of the file body so that the peaks of the folds are flush with the edges of the sides of the file body. Mark the correct position for the tape on both ends of the accordion-folded side.

7 Take the accordion-folded side out of the file body. Cut a strip of double-sided tape to size and press it into place along one end of the accordion-folded side. Remove the tape's

Designer: Terry Taylor

backing and fit the accordion-folded side back into the file body, carefully placing it so that the tape lines up correctly. Attach the other end of the accordion-folded side to the opposite side of the file body the same way.

8 Repeat Steps 6 and 7 to attach the second accordion-folded side to the other end of the file body.

9 Now, make the fasteners using your paper scraps. You'll need two fasteners for each folder. On the files shown in the photo, each fastener consists of a small circle centered over a larger square. You can cut these shapes (or any other) by hand or with decorative paper punches. (To make the next step easier, you may want to secure the small shape to the larger one using a bit of double-sided tape, although this isn't necessary.)

10 You'll attach each fastener to the file body with a brad. Use your craft knife to cut a small slit in each fastener for the brad to fit into. Then, using the project photo as a guide, determine where to place the fasteners on the file. Cut a small slit through the file flap for the upper fastener and one through the file body for the bottom fastener. Place a fastener over a slit on the file; then slip a brad through the slits, spreading the brad's wings on the inside of the file to secure the fastener. Repeat for the remaining fastener.

11 Cut a length of twine, string, or ribbon and wind one end around one of the fasteners.

Paper Day Lilies

Like all origami, this traditional design can be scaled to the size desired.
A bigger piece of paper yields a large flower, while a smaller piece
of paper creates a bud.

materials

Origami paper   Green vellum
Pencil   Floral wire
Craft scissors   Floral tape

Figure 1   Figure 2

Figure 3

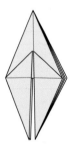

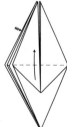

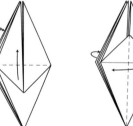

Figure 4   Figure 5   Figure 6

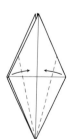

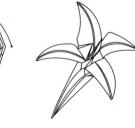

Figure 7   Figure 8   Figure 9

Designer: Rich Maile

step by step

1 Begin with the preliminary fold (see page 135). Now make the frog base by first squash-folding each corner; a squash fold is created as shown in figure 1, folding at the dashed line and pressing open along the fold. A completed squash fold is shown in figure 2.

2 Complete the frog base by petal-folding each side. Make petal folds as indicated in figure 3, folding the bottom of each flap into the center and then opening the folds and pushing the edges to the center. Repeat the folds on each side. You should have four flaps on each side when you've completed the frog base, as in figure 4.

3 To complete the folding of the lily, orient it as shown in figure 5. Mountain-fold the flap as in figure 6, then fold as indicated, as if turning the page in a book. Repeat for each side.

4 Fold each side to the center, as in figure 7. When you've folded each side, as in figure 8, pull the petals down. Use a pencil to curl each petal. The completed lily is shown in figure 9.

5 Cut the leaves from the vellum. Make the stem with the floral wire and use the floral tape to secure the wire to the base of the lily. Cover the wire with the floral tape and finish by wrapping the leaves into place.

Origami Nesting Boxes

Okay, okay, so we're cheating a little. Technically, since you make two scissor cuts, these boxes aren't origami. But they are charming boxes even a beginner can make. Use papers with complementary designs and contrasting textures, and each successive box will reveal a small surprise nestled within.

Designer: Micah Pulleyn

materials

Assorted decorative papers (two pieces for each box: one for the bottom, one for the lid)

Scissors

Bone folder or straight edge (optional)

Pencil

step by step

(Once you've made this box the first time, you'll "get it," and making more will be a cinch. We suggest you practice first with a piece of scrap paper.)

1 Take one sheet of paper. Fold and cut if necessary to make sure you have a perfect square. (You can use a bone folder or straight edge to help you make sharp, straight creases.) Fold this square of paper in half diagonally (corner to corner) to form a triangle, then unfold (figure 1).

2 Fold the paper in half diagonally to form a triangle again, using the opposite corners this time. Once opened, the paper's creases will form an X (figure 2).

3 Fold each corner of the paper into the center so the points meet but do not overlap in the center of the X crease (figures 3 and 4).

4 Unfold the paper to reveal the pattern of creases shown in figure 5. Take one corner of the paper and fold it back into the center again (figure 6). Do not unfold this time. Instead, fold this section of the paper again, so the folded, outside edge meets the crease in the center of the paper (figure 7). Unfold and repeat this procedure with the other three corners.

5 Open the paper and use the pencil to draw four cutting lines on the paper, as shown in figure 8. These lines will make the four corners of the paper now resemble two different

(continues on following page)

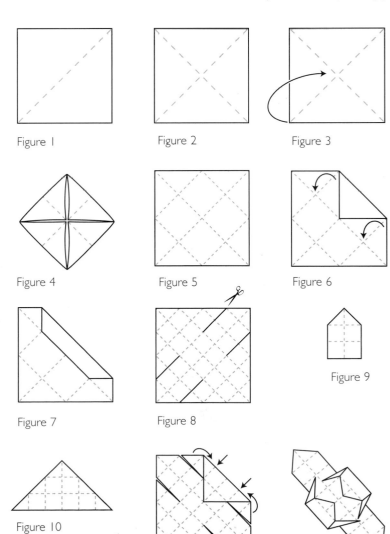

Figure 1

Figure 2

Figure 3

Figure 4

Figure 5

Figure 6

Figure 7

Figure 8

Figure 9

Figure 10

Figure 11

Figure 12

shapes. Two of corners (on opposite sides) will look like houses (figure 9) and the other two will look like mountains (figure 10). It's important to draw the pencil marks accurately and follow them exactly when you cut—don't cut into the square in the center of the paper!

6 Fold both of the mountain-shaped corners so their points touch the center (figure 11). Lift both of these folded edges up to begin forming the box; as you do so, make the two flaps of each mountain shape stand up inside the box (figure 12) so that flaps from opposite sides overlap and touch each other.

7 Use the creases in the house-shaped corners to guide you in folding each of these corners up and over the overlapping flaps to form the box shape. (The "roofs" of the house shapes will complete the bottom of the box.)

8 Repeat Steps 1 through 8 using another piece of paper of the exact same size to make the box lid. To create the boxes that go inside this box, follow the same steps, but use square sheets that are 1 inch smaller each time. (A box made from 12-inch (30.5 cm) square paper can hold a box made from 11-inch (28 cm) square paper, which can hold a box made from 10-inch (25 cm) square paper, etc.)

May Day Fairy Bouquet

Once upon a time, bouquets of flowers had more serious May Day work to do than simply brightening homes and gardens: Superstitious peasants used to adorn their doors and windows with them during May Day celebrations to ward off mischievous fairies! Whether you're looking to fairy-proof your home or simply to make a springtime gift for a friend, this easy project is just the thing.

materials

Sheet of floral-patterned scrapbooking paper

Double-sided tape

Paper doily, 8 inches (20 cm) in diameter

Sheet of leaf- or floral-patterned vellum paper

Button

Thread in a color that matches or complements the papers

Ribbon

Hot-glue gun and glue sticks

Craft knife

Paper clip (optional)

Paper punch

step by step

1 Start by cutting a rectangle measuring 6 x 9 inches (15 x 23 cm) from the floral-patterned scrapbooking paper. Save the scraps for another project.

2 Using the project photo as a guide, roll the rectangle into a cone such that the top edges of the paper meet in a point at the cone's back. Rolling the paper this way will create a nice scooped opening to display the cone's contents.

3 Secure the cone with a strip of double-sided tape on the inside of its seam. (You may find this step easier if you slip a paper clip onto the cone's point first to hold the paper in place while you place the tape.)

4 Roll the paper doily into a cone the same way you rolled the scrapbooking paper in Step 2. Slip the doily cone inside the paper cone and affix it with double-sided tape.

5 Cut three leaves (or flowers) from the vellum paper with your craft knife. Using the photo as a guide, arrange the flowers on the front of the cone and secure them with hot glue.

6 The button on the front of the cone isn't actually sewn in place; it just looks like it is. To achieve this effect, thread your needle with thread that matches or complements the cone and pass it through the buttonholes a few times. Tie off the thread; then glue the button in place on top of the vellum leaves.

7 Use a paper punch to make a hole in the middle of the point at the back of the paper cone. Cut a length of ribbon long enough to suspend the cone and thread it through the hole. Knot the ribbon on the inside of the cone to secure.

8 Fill your May Day "basket" to the brim with fresh, dried, or silk flowers.

tip *Add fragrance to your bouquet by placing a drop or two of your favorite fragrant oil on a dried flower.*

Designer: Susan McBride

Reindeer

This reindeer springs forth from the crane base, one of the basic folds in origami. In addition to the reindeer, many other figures are created from this foundation.

materials

2 sheets of brown origami paper, 6 inches (15 cm) square

Scissors

Clear-drying craft glue

step by step

1 You need to make two crane bases to make the reindeer. Begin with the prelimi-nary fold (page 135). Fold both corners of the top flap to the center and valley-fold the top corner (figure 1). The complet-ed folds are shown in figure 2.

2 Grasp the inside flap at the bottom and pull it up and out, inverting some of the folds (figure 3). Fold into place. Turn over and repeat on the other side to complete the crane base (figure 4). Repeat Steps 1 and 2 to make a sec-ond crane base.

3 Use one crane base to make the reindeer's front section. Begin by inside reverse-folding the tips under,

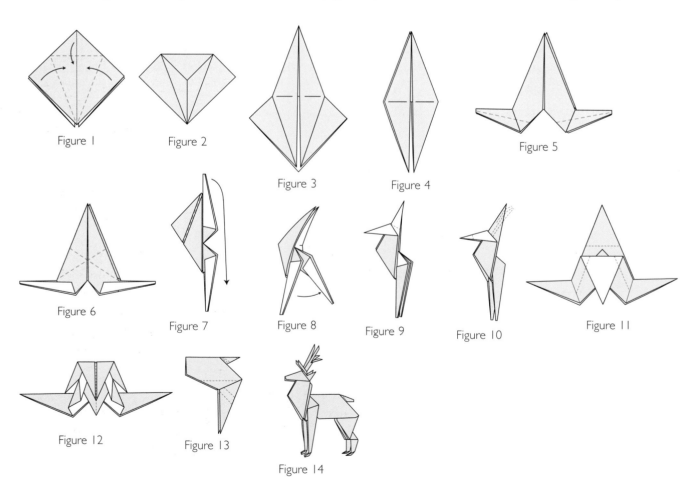

Figure 1

Figure 2

Figure 3

Figure 4

Figure 5

Figure 6

Figure 7

Figure 8

Figure 9

Figure 10

Figure 11

Figure 12

Figure 13

Figure 14

Designer: Rich Maile

then inside reverse-folding the legs (figure 5).

4 Valley-fold as shown in figure 6, folding in numerical order. You'll need to make fold #1, unfold, and then make fold #2 and leave the figure in that position.

5 Mountain- and valley-fold as shown (figure 7), then fold over and pull down the leg (figure 8).

6 Mountain- and valley-fold to form the head, pulling down the outer layer (figure 9). Cut along the dotted lines to make the antlers and fold the nose (figure 10). Fold the antlers and ears as desired.

7 Use the other crane base for the reindeer's rear section. Begin forming the legs by repeating Step 3, but do not fold the tips. Make a valley fold in the top flap and fold down (figure 11). Make valley folds on the

other lines as shown, starting with the sides. The completed folds are shown in figure 12.

8 Now mountain- and valley-fold the body and the tail in half. Fold under the tip of the tail. Tuck under the sides and finish the legs as shown, folding in numerical order (figure 13).

9 To finish the reindeer, glue the sections together (figure 14).

Paper Folding Gallery

Above: Simple shapes of paper were jute-laced together to make these office organizers.
Designer: Terry Taylor

Above right: Always wondering what to do with scraps of holiday gift wrap? Wonder no more — use your scraps to make origami stars for tree ornaments and impromptu gifts.
Designer: Rich Maile

Right: Many handmade papers are flexible enough to stretch and knot with great results. These gift boxes are almost too pretty to open!
Designer: Marie McConville

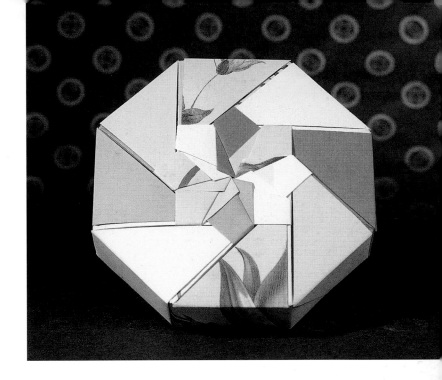

Below: The vellum lotus blossom embellishment on the front of this card unfolds to reveal an envelope ideal for charms or mementos.
Designer: Annie Cicale

Above top and above: The appeal of these intriguing origami boxes was enhanced by using paper with printed flower and bird motifs instead of traditional origami paper.
Designer: Rich Maile

Left: Corrugated cardboard adds interesting texture to these gift boxes. Decorative bows and embellishments complete the look.
Designer: Marie McConville

Paper Mache
& Paper Clay

Remember the messy paper mache projects you made as a school child? Well, forget them! Crafting technology has developed two great alternatives: paper clay and instant paper mache, both of which can be molded, shaped, and painted with fabulous results.

materials

paper clay

Sold in premixed packages, this white clay is durable, flexible, and fun to work with.

instant paper mache

Sold in both white and natural gray, this paper pulp product is lightweight and sold in large bags. Just add water to mix.

plastic wrap

Everyday kitchen wrap protects work surfaces and helps ensure smooth, even clay and mache.

plastic freezer bags

Why dirty a bowl and your hands? Knead your instant paper mache with water in a plastic bag for maximum efficiency and minimal cleanup.

rolling pin

Wood or plastic rolling pins help roll paper clay and instant paper mache into smooth, pliable textures.

foam and wood bases

Virtually any simple shape can be covered with instant paper mache or paper clay.

clay tools

An inexpensive set of clay tools will serve you well in all sorts of unanticipated ways, creating special effects as well as basic shapes.

craft knife & embroidery needle

A craft knife and an embroidery needle can accomplish many of the same tasks as clay tools.

fine sandpaper

Paper clay projects should be gently sanded for an ultr-fine surface.

face mask

Prevent fine paper particles from entering your lungs while sanding by wearing a face mask. An inexpensive, disposable mask is fine.

acrylic paints

You can add color to your paper clay and mache projects in several ways. The clay and mache dough can be tinted when you first begin handling it by simply adding a little paint and mixing it in until you're happy with the amount of color. You can also paint the finished projects. Experiment to create special effects by mixing color with iridescent paints or adding a little glitter to your paint.

basic techniques

instant paper mache

Instant paper mache is a flexible alternative to traditional newspaper and paste paper mache. The paper pulp is easy to work with — just add water — and the finished texture can be as smooth or rough as you like.

1 Place the mache mixture in a plastic freezer bag. Add the amount of warm water directed by the manufacturer.

2 Knead the water and pulp together in the bag on a dry surface until all of the dry spots disappear.

3 Adjust the texture if necessary by adding additional water or dry mache mixture.

basic techniques

4 For a smooth finish, roll the mache mixture to an even thickness between two sheets of plastic wrap.

For a rough finish, work the mache mixture over a foam, wood, or cardboard base.

paper clay

Paper clay is fun to work with, yet doesn't require any special handling or firing like ceramic clay. When prepared as directed below, virtually any shape with any type of pattern can be cut out of the clay.

1 Flatten about half a package of clay with your palms into an oval shape.

2 Place the oval disk between two sheets of plastic wrap and use a rolling pin or cylinder to roll the clay flat. One-eigth to $3/16$ inch (6 to 9 mm) is a common thickness, but always refer to your project directions for the specific thickness needed.

3 After each pass with the rolling pin, peel back the plastic wrap and reposition the clay to prevent sticking. Check the size and shape of the slab as you roll, keeping the size and shape of your pattern in mind.

4 Peel back the top layer of plastic wrap and place your pattern on top of the clay.

5 Cut around the pattern using a craft knife or a clay knife tool.

6 Carefully smooth out the clay surfaces with your fingertips, sprinkling on a little water if needed.

7 Wearing a face mask, gently sand any rough edges using sandpaper when the clay has dried. Wipe the surfaces free of dust.

Paper Clay Dragonflies

Most crafters have a favorite icon that they use in everything from handcrafted cards to scrapbooking pages to journal covers. Paper clay is a great medium to recreate those images in three dimensions, and the decorative possibilities are almost unlimited.

materials

8-ounce (227 g) package of paper clay

Plastic kitchen wrap

Rolling pin or cylinder

Craft knife or clay knife tool

Embroidery needle or clay piercing tool

Paper napkins

Fine sandpaper

Face mask

Acrylic paint in colors of your choice

Iridescent white paint (optional)

Medium and fine paintbrushes

Thin-gauge craft wire

2 beads in size and color of your choice

Jewelry or craft pliers

Wire cutters

step by step

1 Photocopy the dragonfly shapes on page 314, enlarging or reducing if desired.

2 Flatten a piece of paper clay between two sheets of plastic wrap and use a rolling pin or cylinder to roll the clay to about $3/16$ inch (4.5 mm) thickness. If the clay sticks to the plastic wrap, peel back the plastic wrap and reposition the clay in between rollings.

3 Peel back the top layer of plastic wrap. Place the dragonfly pattern on the clay and cut around the pattern using a clay knife tool or a craft knife.

4 Remove the paper clay scraps and carefully smooth out the top and bottom edges and surfaces of the dragonfly. Use a little water if needed. Note: Avoid the temptation to cut out multiple dragonflies at the same time to prevent the clay from drying out.

5 Using a needle tool, poke a hole through the center of the dragonfly while the clay is still soft.

6 Use folded cotton or paper napkins to prop up the wings of the dragonflies while the clay dries. Allow the clay to completely dry.

7 Wearing a facemask, carefully sand any rough edges using sandpaper. Wipe the surfaces free of dust.

8 Paint your dragonflies a solid color. For a more lustrous look, blend your paints with a little iridescent white paint before using. Allow the paint to completely dry, then add decorative accents in a contrasting color, referring to the photo as a guide.

9 Cut a 4-inch (10 cm) length of wire. Bend the top $1/4$ inch (6 mm) of the wire into a small loop. Secure the loop

Designer: Kelly McMullen

closed by twisting the end of the wire around the loop several times. Trim off any excess wire.

10 Slide your beads onto the wire so they rest against the loop, then insert the wire into the hole you made in the clay in Step 6.

11 Working on the back side of the dragonfly, pull the wire end until the beads rest snugly against the front side. Trim the wire on the back side to ¼ inch, then wrap it around the top of your pliers to create a spiral.

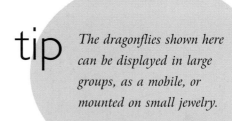

tip *The dragonflies shown here can be displayed in large groups, as a mobile, or mounted on small jewelry.*

Paper Clay Magnets

Express your personality in vibrant colors with refrigerator art! These magnets are simple to make, and can be cut in any shape or size desired. Consider heart shapes for Valentine's Day, snowflakes or trees for the winter holidays, or pumpkins for Halloween.

materials

8-ounce (227 g) package of paper clay

Plastic wrap

Rolling pin or cylinder

Craft knife or clay knife tool

Fine sandpaper

Face mask

Acrylic paint in colors of your choice

Iridescent white paint (optional)

Fine paintbrushes

Magnets

Clear-drying craft glue

step by step

1 Tear off a small piece of paper clay and flatten it between your palms. Place the disk between two sheets of plastic wrap and use a rolling pin or cylinder to roll the clay to about ⅛ inch (3 mm) thick. If necessary, peel back the plastic wrap and reposition the clay to prevent sticking.

2 Peel back the top layer of plastic wrap. Use a circle of pleasing size (at least as large as the diameter of the magnet) as a pattern. The magnets shown here were made using the top of a large glue stick. Place the circle pattern on the clay and cut around the pattern using a clay knife tool or a craft knife.

3 Remove paper clay scraps and carefully smooth out the surfaces of the circles, sprinkling on a little water if needed. Allow the clay to completely dry.

4 Wearing a face mask, carefully sand any rough edges using sandpaper when the clay has dried. Wipe the surfaces free of dust.

5 Paint your circles a solid color, then add decorative accents in contrasting colors. For a more lustrous look, blend your acrylic paints with iridescent white paint before using.

6 Glue the magnet to the back of the disk.

Designer: Kelly McMullen

Stamped Paper Mache Name Plaque

This paper mache plaque playfully announces that you are entering children's territory, and can be customized to match any child's room décor.

materials

Wax paper

Instant paper mache

Bowl and water

Dishwashing liquid

Basting brush

Rolling pin

Waxed paper

Cardboard form

Butter knife

Bead, button, or stamp with decorative surface

Alphabet stamps

Drying rack

Acrylic paints

Varnish

Brush

Ribbon

Felt

step by step

1 Following manufacturer's instructions, mix paper mache with water. Knead mixture until it achieves the consistency of bread dough, adding more paper mache to the mixture if it's too sticky or more water if it's too dry.

2 Pour a few tablespoons of dishwashing liquid into a small bowl and dilute it with a small amount of water. This mixture will be used to smooth the surface of the paper mache mixture.

3 Remove a lump of the paper mache mixture and form it into a large ball. Place the ball between two sheets of wax paper and roll until flat.

4 Lay the cardboard form on the flattened paper mache mixture, and use the butter knife to cut around the form, leaving an additional ½ inch (1.25 cm) of paper mache around the form. Remove the extraneous paper mache mixture from your work surface

5 Carefully fold the flattened paper mache mixture around the cardboard form.

6 Create a decorative frame border by pressing a bead, button, or stamp with a decorative surface around the edge of the paper mache-covered form. To prevent sticking, dip the bead, button, or stamp into the detergent/water mixture between each use.

7 Use the alphabet stamps the same way to create an impression of the child's name on the paper mache-covered form.

8 Create other shapes or figures if desired with any excess mache mixture and gently press them into the form. If they don't stay in place, lightly wet the mache form and try again. This designer added flowers, stems, and leaf figures.

9 Lift the form with a spatula and place on a

Designer: Megan Kirby

rack to dry. Allow to completely
dry overnight.

10 Paint the frame and any shapes or figures you added with acrylic paint and allow to completely dry.

11 Add a finishing coat of varnish and allow to completely dry. Cover with a coat of varnish and allow to completely dry.

12 Cut a length of ribbon and thread it through the paper mache holes at the top of the frame, then tie a hanging bow at the top to finish.

Spring Fling

These colorful blooms are easy to craft with paper clay. Display them in large groups, as a bouquet, or tie single blooms onto gift tags and bows. To create slight variations in the size of the flowers, start with larger or smaller pieces of clay.

materials

8-ounce (227 g) package of paper clay

Acrylic paint in colors of your choice (green for the stems and a lighter and darker color for the blooms)

Iridescent white paint

Small paintbrushes

Bamboo skewers

Small glass jars (See Step 5)

Fine sandpaper

Face mask

Acrylic paint in colors of your choice

Iridescent white paint (optional)

Designer: Kelly McMullen

step by step

1 Tear off a piece of paper clay approximately the size of a large green grape. Use your fingers to flatten the ball into a flower shape, beginning with an indentation in the center and flatten into a disk from the center outward. The disk should be thicker in the center and gradually become thinner at the edges as it flattens and expands in diameter, with the edges very thin and uneven.

2 Use your fingernail to score the center of the circle, then shape the disk into a slight cup.

3 Tear off a pea-sized piece of clay and form it into a cylinder. Attached the flat/large side of the cylinder to the outside of the flower, and join it firmly to the center of the flower to form a base.

4 Press the flat end of a skewer into the center of the flower base to form a hole. Remove the skewer for now.

5 Use a jar with an opening smaller than the circumference of the flowers to mold the disk into a cup shape as it dries. (Old spice jars work very well.) With the flower's base side facing downward, press the flower into the top of the spice jar so the flower forms a pleasing shape. Allow the clay to completely dry.

6 Wearing a face mask, carefully sand any rough edges with fine sandpaper. Wipe the surfaces free of dust.

7 Blend your acrylic paints with iridescent white paint, then paint the flower petals. Multiple layers will create a more natural, visually interesting look. Paint the center a darker color.

8 For each flower, paint a skewer green and allow to completely dry.

9 Place a dot of glue on the end of the skewer and insert it into the hole in the base. Allow to completely dry.

No-Throw, No-Fire, All-Fabulous Tissue Paper Bowl

Why should potters have all the fun? With this simple technique, you can create bowls every bit as fabulous looking (and not nearly as breakable) as anything a ceramist can throw. Just don't try eating your breakfast cereal out of it!

materials

Ceramic or plastic bowl for mold

Plastic grocery bag

Clothespin or binder clip

Packet of tissue paper

1–2 sheets of vellum paper

White craft glue

Paintbrush

Craft knife

step by step

1 Start by wrapping the ceramic bowl in the plastic grocery bag, making sure that the bottom of the bowl rests in the bottom of the bag. Pull the bag taut around the top of the bowl, twist the bag's opening closed, and secure it with the clothespin or binder clip. This plastic-wrapped bowl will serve as the form for your tissue paper bowl.

2 Separate the packet of tissue paper into stacks that are thin enough to cut cleanly with scissors. Cut these stacks into strips about 2 inches (5 cm) wide and long enough to drape over the bowl with a little extra at each end. Separate the individual sheets from each strip so that you have a pile of strips, each just one paper thick.

3 Place the plastic-covered bowl on your work surface, open end down and dome up. Drape a strip of tissue paper over the bowl's dome. Dip your paintbrush in white craft glue and apply a thorough coat of glue to the strip. Drape a second strip of tissue paper over the bowl and paint it with glue the same way. Continue applying strips until you've covered the entire bowl with one layer.

4 Apply at least five more layers of tissue paper strips in the same manner. Allow the bowl to partially dry.

5 To decorate the bowl, cut the vellum into several sizes of the same shape. The project shown features open rectangles with rounded corners. Arrange the shapes on the bowl as desired, then glue them in place just as you glued the strips.

6 Apply a final coat of glue to the entire bowl and allow it to dry for at least 24 hours. Trim any ragged paper ends at the bowl's edges with a craft knife.

7 To release the paper bowl from the form, untie the plastic bag and remove the

Designer: Kathryn Temple

ceramic bowl from inside of it. Carefully pull the plastic bag away from the tissue paper bowl. The inside of the paper bowl may require a little extra drying time.

 tip

The same technique can be used to create vessels of almost any shape. Vases, china pieces, and everday serving dishes are good sources for molds.

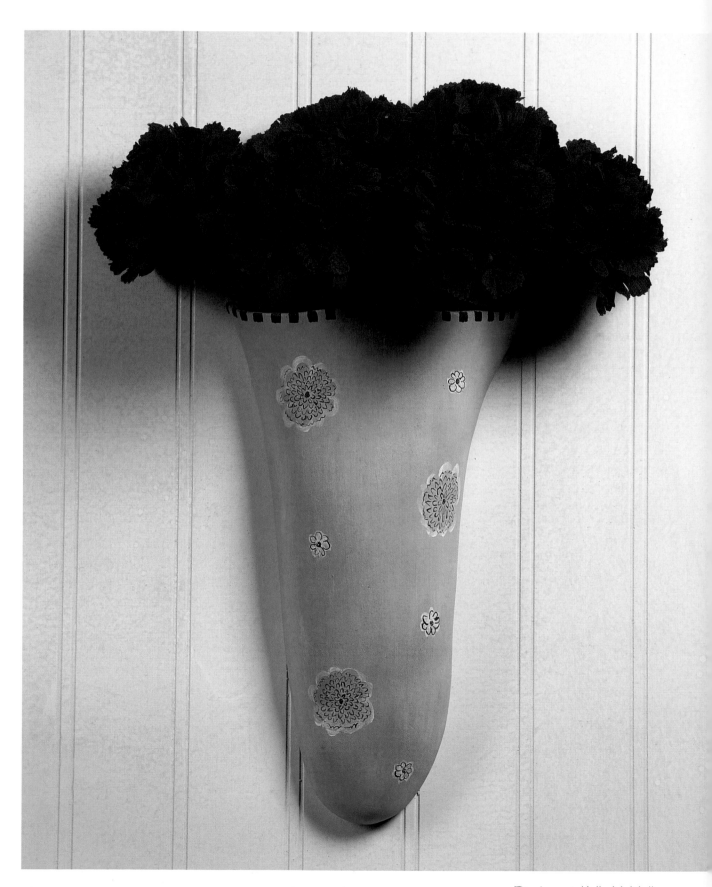

Designer: Kelly McMullen

Wall Vase

The simple shape of this wall vase makes it a great first project if you're new to paper clay. To display, just fill the vase with dried or silk flowers; or, if you prefer fresh flowers, place their stems first in a smaller vase or in water tubes.

materials

8-ounce (227 g) package of paper clay

Plastic wrap

Rolling pin or cylinder

Craft knife or clay knife tool

Embroidery needle or clay piercing tool

Cotton/paper napkins

Fine sandpaper

Face mask

Acrylic paint in colors of your choice

Iridescent white paint (optional)

Medium and fine paintbrushes

step by step

1 Photocopy top and bottom vase shapes on pages 312 and 313 and set aside.

2 Flatten about half a packageounces of clay with your palms into an oval shape about ½ inch (12 mm) or less thick.

3 Place the disk between two sheets of plastic wrap and use a rolling pin or cylinder to roll the clay to about ⅛- to 3⁄16-inch (6 to 9 mm) thickness. After each pass with the rolling pin, peel back the plastic wrap and reposition the clay to prevent sticking. Check the size and shape of the slab as you roll and adjust your rolling to ensure that the slab will accommodate the vase shape.

4 Peel back the top layer of plastic wrap and place the top vase pattern on the clay. Cut around the pattern using a craft knife or a clay knife tool.

5 Remove paper clay scraps and carefully smooth out the surfaces of the vase piece, sprinkling on a litter water if needed.

6 Repeat Steps 2 through 5 for the bottom of the vase.

7 Using a needle tool, make a hole through the top center of the vase back while the clay is still soft.

8 Carefully place the top slab against the bottom slab, bending the top piece so that the edges abut the edges of the bottom piece. Gently press the edges together and smooth them to form a solid seal. Adjust the shape and curve as desired while the clay is still supple. Use cotton or crumbled paper napkins if necessary to prop up the top in a nice curve.

9 Wearing a face mask, carefully sand any rough edges using sandpaper when the clay has dried. Wipe the surfaces free of dust.

10 Use acrylic paint to paint the surface a solid color, then add decorative accents in a contrasting color if desired. For a more lustrous look, blend the paints with iridescent white paint before using.

Paper Mache Seashells

Instant paper mache can be molded into great shapes with candy and soap molds to create one-of-a kind embellishments and tree ornaments. In this project, molded seashells were glued onto paper mache boxes, then painted and antiqued.

materials

Instant paper mache

Paper mache boxes

Large sealable plastic bag

Candy mold

Liquid dish detergent

Fine sandpaper

Clear-drying craft glue

Craft knife

Fork

Creamy white, white-white, and
  burnt umber acrylic paints

Paintbrush

Clear varnish

Paper towel

step by step

1 Mix the paper mache and water according to the manufacturer's instructions, kneading well to achieve a smooth consistency.

2 Lightly grease your candy mold with a layer of dish detergent diluted with water.

Press the mache mixture a little at a time into the molds with enough pressure to make sure it goes into the grooves. Allow to completely dry.

3 Remove your mache shapes from the molds. Sand the bottoms lightly if necessary so they will sit level on the box tops.

4 Trim the edges of the shapes if necessary with a craft knife, then glue them to the center top of the boxes.

5 To decorate the sides of the boxes, make 8 small balls and a 10-inch-long (25 cm) snake of mache. Press them in place against the sides of the boxes, then add texture with a fork. Allow to completely dry.

6 Paint the bottom and tops of the boxes with several

coats of creamy white paint, allowing the paint to completely dry in between coats.

7 Dilute the white-white paint with water. Brush it on the box bottoms and tops, then blot it off with a paper towel to create the illusion of depth. Allow the paint to completely dry.

8 Apply a coat of clear acrylic varnish to the boxes and allow to completely dry.

9 Mix a small mount of burnt umber paint with varnish. Brush it on the boxes, then lightly blot lightly with a paper towel.

Designer: Chris Rankin

Paper Mache & Paper Clay Gallery

Top: Celebrate the holiday season with Victorian Santas molded with instant paper mache! Make miniature versions for tree ornaments and larger ornaments for tabletop decorations.
Designer: Mary Beth Ruby

Above: Finger puppets are easy to create with instant paper mache. Just form a rough base from crushed aluminum foil and shape the mache around it. Shop the scrapbooking aisle for embellishments and have fun creating unique personalities.
Designer: Dana Irwin

Above: Instant paper mache and a foam core provided the base for this whimsical clock. The playful textures and patterns were created with soft mache and acrylic paints.
Designer: Diane L. Weaver

Above: Your image of newspaper and paste mache may date back to grade school when you used it to make globes and volcanoes. Fortunately, the grown-up world is much more fun! This vase was made by layering newspaper mache over a purchased glass container, which was then painted and gessoed.
Designer: Anne McCloskey

Left: The stamped effect on this vase was created by applying flower cutouts to a paper mached vase form, then covering the vase with thin Asian paper with decoupage medium.
Designer: Terry Taylor

Collage

Got the urge to create a work of art but lack the drawing skills of Picasso or Matisse? Try a slightly more democratic medium that was practiced by both of those great artists— collage. This very personal form of expression is equally at home adorning the walls of an art gallery or a lampshade.

materials

collage material

Typically, collages are categorized as paper, fabric, mixed media, or found objects. What this really means is that practically anything can (and has) been used to create collages. See Collage Material at right for a list of possible collage materials.

adhesives

You'll need different adhesives depending on the collage material you plan to use. White craft glue (PVA glue) is acid-free and non-toxic and it works well for most papers.

ACRYLIC MEDIUM (available under various brand names) is often used as both an adhesive and a sealant for collage; it comes in a mat or gloss finish. See Applying Adhesives on page 178.

WHITE CRAFT GLUE is another popular choice for creating layers of decorative papers. White craft glue is generally not a good choice for attaching heavy or nonpaper items.

GLUE STICKS work well for small intricate collages. If you're using very delicate papers, consider using rubber cement, which won't soak or wrinkle the papers, but keep in mind that it can lose its hold eventually.

AEROSOL ADHESIVES are another option, but they should be used only in well-ventilated areas.

EPOXY RESINS (one part adhesive, one part hardener/catalyst) work well for attaching heavier objects to a collage or assemblage. Depending on the surface to which you are attaching your collage, staples, screws, nails, colored tacks, ropes and chains can all be used as fasteners. Consider leaving such hardware exposed as a part of your collage design.

craft knife & scissors

When cutting out collage material, use a good pair of regular scissors to cut away large areas and small manicure or embroidery scissors to clip very small or intricate designs. A craft knife (with a supply of sharp blades) works best for cutting very straight lines and some detail work.

cutting mat

Use a self-healing cutting mat to protect your work surface when using a craft knife. A piece of non-corrugated cardboard can be used as an inexpensive alternative.

paint brushes

You'll need these in a range of sizes: small artist brushes for embellishing your collage and larger brushes for applying medium or painting your collage surface.

metal ruler

This serves as a straightedge for cutting and tearing.

brayer

This tool is similar to a small paint roller but is made of rubber. Use it to press out bubbles or wrinkles before your adhesive dries. A small wallpaper smoother can be used instead of a brayer.

access to a photocopier

Using a photocopier will allow you to use one-of-a-kind items, such as cherished photographs, in your collages without destroying the originals. It will also let you enlarge or reduce the image, or (if you copy it in black and white) also alter its colors.

sticker machine

While not required for collage work, these nifty machines (available at craft stores) can apply permanent or repositionable adhesive to paper, fabric, or other materials less than $1/16$th-inch thick (1.6 mm), eliminating the need for glue or other adhesives. (See sidebar on page 178.)

basic techniques

preparing surfaces

Almost any surface can be embellished with collage, but you may need to invest a few minutes to make the surface more receptive to adhesives.

1 Use warm water and mild detergent to thoroughly clean the surface of the object to be collage. Let the object dry completely. Sand wood surfaces. Use steel wool to remove rust from metal, then clean the surface with a solution of half vinegar and half water.

2 All porous objects need to be sealed with a sealant or varnish before being collaged. Prime wood objects to prepare them for painting, or seal them if you don't plan to paint them. Metal surfaces should be primed with a suitable product; apply rust-proofing sealant for additional protection. Gesso can be painted on clean objects to cre-

ate a smooth surface for collaging. Apply five thin coats in alternating directions following the manufacturer's directions.

3 If you want to paint the object before applying collage papers, paint several thin coats rather than a single thick one. Sand lightly between coats and then one final time with fine sandpaper.

collage material

Just about anything you can get to stick to a surface can be used in collage. Here's a list to get you started:

wrapping paper

purchased specialty papers

magazine, newspaper, and catalogue cutouts

postage stamps

postcards

calendars

greeting cards

stationery

prints from old books

wallpaper

movie and show tickets

maps

sheet music

jigsaw puzzle pieces

fabric scraps

lace

ribbon

yarn

string

leather scraps

felt

buttons

pressed flowers

dried natural materials

metal scraps

beads

food labels

Go Digital!

The Internet is a great source for collage images. Download images onto your computer and print them out on a color printer. Seal your printouts with acrylic medium before using.

basic techniques

cutting paper for collage

All it takes is practice and a little patience to clip perfect cutouts for your collages.

applying adhesives

Plan to experiment a little a little experimentation to figure out which adhesives work best with which your favorite collage materials. Here are some guidelines for applying the most commonly used adhesives.

1 To apply white craft glue (PVA glue) or acrylic

medium, water the substance down slightly with water (acrylic medium can be used full strength) and brush it onto the surface where you intend to place the cut collage material. Another option is to brush the watered-down glue onto back side of your collage papers.

2 Press the collage material into place on top of the glue, using your fingers or a small brayer to gently work out any air bubbles or wrinkles. Small wrinkles that add texture to the work can be left as part of your design.

sealing your collage

Both acrylic medium and white craft glue can be brushed onto the top of your completed collage to act as a sealant. White craft glue is milky when applied, but it will dry clear and hard.

Sticker Machines

Making a collage is all about changing your mind: arranging and rearranging. That's why the latest tool to sweep the craft world, the sticker/lamination machine can be a collage artist's best friend. This simple machine will apply a layer of repositionable adhesive to the back of your paper or fabric, so you can use the trial-and-error method and create a collage instead of a mess. (See page 10 for more information.)

To use one for collage, simply cut out your desired image or images, make sure you have the correct cartridge in the machine, and then run your material face up

through the machine to apply repositionable adhesive to its back. (You can arrange several small items in the machine's input tray at once so as not to waste cartridge material.) After that, it's a matter of peeling the item from the adhesive paper and arranging and rearranging your items on the collage surface.

basic techniques

the art of composing

Most collage artists believe that the process of making the collage is as important as the final outcome. Spontaneity and the happy accidents that occur from play are all a part of this art form, so let yourself relax and have fun when composing your collages. Here are a few tips to help you get started with design basics.

Arranging and rearranging and then re-rearranging are what creating a collage is all about, so don't get discouraged: changing your mind, adjusting, and fine-tuning are all part of the process. Remember that each time you add or remove an item the balance of the entire collage will be altered, so don't permanently glue anything down until you're certain of its placement.

Layering is an important aspect of most collage design. Layering allows your design to build on itself. It also permits you to cover over unsuccessful areas or to tear off layers to "rediscover" what lies beneath.

The focal point is the spot that first engages the eye and draws it into the collage's design. Creating a focal point is usually a simple matter of finding one extra interesting image that dominates the design. This becomes a kind of visual rest stop that the eye returns to each time it explores the collage.

Repetition is a simple way to create unity in your design. Using objects with similar shapes, colors, or textures in your collage will help link disparate areas to produce a feeling of cohesion.

Variety keeps a design from looking static. Making changes in the scale, color, or texture can provide the contrasts that make a collage come alive.

Color can be used to balance your design. In general, a mix of light and dark colors works best in collages. Too much of one color will usually make a piece look unbalanced or result in one area of the collage blending together and "disappearing."

Step back from your work while composing, both literally and figuratively. Consider whether your collage will be viewed up close or from far away. When viewed from a distance, some areas of your collage may blend together and become "blank spots." If this happens, you'll need to add a larger item or a contrasting color or shape in that space. You may also find yourself wondering when your collage is done or if you've added so much that it's overdone. If this is the case, put it away for a while and come back to it when you can see it with "fresh" eyes.

Collage Confidence

The trick to creating random collage effects is to work in stages. Start with shapes spaced well apart from each other, then fill in the blank spaces as desired. It's far easier to add elements to the design than take them away!

Inspired Tea Tray

In many Asian cultures, food service is an art form. Enjoy some of that same artistry during your own tea times with this handsome decoupage and collage serving tray.

materials

Embroidery thread

Beads

4 flat paintbrushes, 1 inch (2.5 cm) wide

Ruler or measuring tape

Scissors

step by step

1 Start by preparing the wooden serving tray. Sand it well, then wipe it clean with a damp cloth. Allow the tray to air dry for a few minutes.

2 The tray in the photo features several recessed compartments, which have been painted white. If your tray has similar compartments, paint them first. You may need to apply several coats of paint to achieve the desired intensity of color. If so, allow the paint to dry thoroughly between each coat and sand lightly before applying the next coat.

3 When the white paint has dried thoroughly, paint the exterior and inside sides of the tray red, masking the white areas of the tray to prevent splatters. Apply multiple coats, if necessary, sanding between applications.

4 When the final coat of paint is completely dry, apply the gold accents to the handles and short sides of the box. You can do this either by decoupaging them with gold paper or by using gold leaf. If you're using gold leaf, simply follow the manufacturer's instructions.

5 To decoupage the handles and sides, start by cutting the gold paper into appropriately sized strips. Spread a thin layer of glue or decoupage medium over a small portion of one of the handles, using one of the smaller paintbrushes. Then carefully press a paper strip into place, using your fingers to smooth away any bubbles. Repeat until you've covered both handles with gold. Apply a thin coat of decoupage medium to the handles and allow it to dry completely.

6 The design inside the tray is created by decoupaging a collage inside each recessed compartment. Start by making the col-

(continues on following page)

Designer: Megan Kirby

lages: Measure the area to be decoupaged. Then, from the white paper, measure and cut a piece to fit each compartment.

7 On each piece of paper you cut in Step 6, create a collage from your photos, magazine cutouts, and other Asian-themed ephemera. Spend some time arranging the images before gluing them into place. Then allow the glue to dry.

8 Spread a thin layer of glue over the serving surface of the tray and to the back of each collage. Press the collages into place, smoothing away any bubbles with your fingers. Allow the glue to dry; then apply a coat of decoupage medium over the collages and let it dry.

9 Finally, make the two tassels. For each tassel, cut 20 to 25 6-inch (15 cm) lengths of embroidery thread and two 10-inch (25 cm) lengths. Gather the 6-inch (15 cm) lengths into a bundle, making sure that their ends are even. Secure the bundle of threads by tying and knotting one of the longer lengths of thread around its center.

10 Fold the bundle in half and tie the second 10-inch length around it, about half an inch below the top of the fold. Trim the ends of this second length so that they're even with the threads in the bundle.

11 String beads onto each end of the first 10-inch (25 cm) length, securing them with a tiny dab of glue. Allow the glue to dry; then tie the tassels onto the tray's handles.

Garden in a Box

Packed with seeds selected from your personal favorites, this simple project would make a lovely housewarming gift for a new neighbor. Make an extra box or two for yourself and bring beautiful organization to your potting bench.

materials

Cardboard box and top

Gold spray paint

Decorative papers in various floral motifs

Decoupage medium, glossy or clear-drying craft glue

4 wooden beads

Butterfly shaped or other decorative garden-inspired beads

Small paper bags

Flower seeds

Scissors

Craft brush

Pencil

Flower stamps

Label stamp

Stamp pad

Black marker

Designer: Megan Kirby

step by step

1 Working in a well-ventilated area and following the paint manufacturer's instructions, spray the inside of the cardboard box with the gold paint. Allow the paint to completely dry.

2 In the project shown, each side of the box and the box top are covered with a different floral paper. To re-create this look, start by deciding which paper you'd like for each surface. Trace each surface onto the paper you've selected for it. (Simply place the box on the paper and trace around its edge with a pencil.) Then cut along the pencil lines and trim the paper to size.

3 Using the craft brush, spread a thin, even layer of decoupage medium or glue on the back of one of the sheets you cut in Step 2. Press the sheet into place on the box, smoothing away any bubbles with your fingers.

4 Repeat Step 3 until you've covered all the sides of the box and the box top. Then brush a thin layer of decoupage medium or clear-drying craft glue over the entire box and the box top.

5 When the box has dried completely, add additional decorative elements: bits of decorative paper, garden-inpired beads, dried flowers, or stamps,

for instance. Then apply a final layer of decoupage medium and let it dry.

6 Add legs to the boxby gluing a wooden bead to each corner of the bottom.

7 Next, decorate each bag, using the label and flower stamps and bits of decorative paper.

8 Use the black marker to label the bags, then fill each bag with seeds according to its label. For a nice touch, include planting instructions on the backs of the bags.

Paper Collection Altered Book Pages

Paper dolls, cancelled stamps…everyone has a little box of interesting paper goods that they don't quite know how to display. With this project, you can turn your collection of 1930's movie-star photos into a fabulous coffee table display. Make several collections, and alternate them on your coffee table. A great way to store your collections, too!

materials

Blank or printed book

Acrylic medium

Paintbrush

Bone folder

Packs of collage paper and scrapbook paper

Waxed paper

Magazines, vintage catalogs and newspapers, your 'collection'

Scissors

Rubber stamp alphabet (or other lettering)

Sticker machine

step by step

1   Choose the dimensions of the book carefully. You'll want your biggest piece to fit comfortably on the page, and all of the pieces to fit in the book.

2   Brush a thin, even coat of acrylic medium onto one of the pages in the book. Press two pages together, and use a bone folder to smooth out air pockets or wrinkles. On the back side of the two pages, brush on another thin, even coat of acrylic medium, and press a third page onto the previous two. Paste three or four pages together in this manner, as this will help make each group sturdy.

3   Skip a page, then repeat Step 2 to form a second stack of pages.

4   Cut decorative paper to use as the background for each page to be altered. Adhere the paper to each facing page with a thin coat of acrylic medium, smoothing with the bone folder to remove air pockets and wrinkles.

5   Place sheets of waxed paper between each group of glued pages, close the book, and stack several heavy books on top. Allow your book to dry completely, usually overnight.

6   Cut out your images, then play with different arrangements until you're happy with the look. Use a sticker machine to adhere them together and to the page. The project shown features pictures of hats from a vintage catalog found at a flea market.

7   For an optional flair, add text to your pages, using rubber stamps or other lettering materials. When all your pages are filled, embellish the cover as desired.

Designer: Terry Taylor

Tissue Paper Collage

Sometimes, you just don't know what that jumble of thoughts bumping around in your head means until you spend some time taking it apart and piecing it back together again in your journal. Collage works the same way: With a little time (and some glue!), you can fit all those crazy pieces together into a beautiful, meaningful design.

materials

Paper and pencil for sketching
Variety of tissue papers
Blank journal
Decoupage medium, matte finish
Colored pencils and/or pens
Paintbrush
Scissors
Craft knife

step by step

1 If you'd like, start by sketching the design for your collage. Making a sketch of what you'd like to represent with your collage can help you choose a color palette and guide how you'll cut or tear your tissue pieces.

2 Choose a color of tissue paper to use as the base for your collage. You can think of it as an "under-painting" for your design. Tear the paper into pieces measuring about 2 inches (5 cm) square. For more control and cleaner edges, you

can use a craft knife to cut the pieces instead.

3 Paint a thin, even layer of decoupage medium over the journal's cover, then pat the squares of tissue paper from Step 2 in place to cover the entire surface. Be sure to cover the journal's edges, too — just fold the pieces of paper over them and brush some decoupage medium on top to affix. Spread another thin layer of decoupage medium over the now-papered surface and allow it to dry thoroughly.

4 Now, start work on the design. You can tear or cut all your tissue pieces at once, or do so as you work to make sure you have the right sizes.

5 To add a layer of your design on top of the base color, simply apply decoupage medium where you'd like to add the next color, and press the tissue pieces into place.

6 Allow the decoupage medium to dry thoroughly between each layer of color you add: Not only will tissue paper rip and smear if you overwork it, but tissue paper colors are more intense when they're wet, making it difficult to judge how your design is progressing until it's dry.

7 When you're finished layering your design and the journal has dried completely, you may wish to define certain elements with colored pencils or pen work. The fence on the journal cover shown, for instance, is drawn on in ink.

Designer: Susan McBride

Collage Lamp Shade

Why should scrapbookers and card makers have all the fun? The die-cut machines so popular with those crafters can be used to make great lamp shades, also. Choose animal shapes for a fun children's lamp or swirls for a more contemporary look.

materials

Ivory or white lamp shade

Collage paper

Handmade paper

Die-cut machine

Acrylic medium

Paintbrush

Raffia

Tapestry needle

step by step

1 To give your lamp shade a unified design, cut and tear papers into small (about 2 inches or 5 cm) squares. Tear some of the squares into strips.

2 Cut designs in several of your squares with a die-cut machine. Swirl shapes were used in this project.

3 Working on a small area of the lampshade at a time, brush a coat of acrylic medium onto the area you are working, then press shapes onto the shade, smoothing each shape by patting it lightly with a clean brush or a lightly moistened fingertip. Allow some space between the shapes when you begin, then begin overlapping shapes as desired.

4 When you've worked your way around the shade and you're happy with the look, brush the shade with a thin, sealing coat of acrylic medium. Allow this coat to completely dry.

5 Thread the raffia onto a tapestry needle and whipstitch around the top and bottom rims of the shade, leaving a loose end about 2 inches long. If you run out of raffia as you stitch, just knot another strand onto the end of the sewn strand, placing the knots on the interior of the shade.

6 When you meet the loose end of the raffia, tie the ends together in a knot, positioning it on the interior of the shade.

tip

Paper sheer enough for light to pass through creates lovely effects when the lamp is turned on, so hold your prospective paper up to a light source before making a final choice.

Designer: Terry Taylor

Clothesline Collage

Save those scraps! Even the smallest leftovers from your scrapbooking and card making projects can make great additions to collage projects. The paper clothing in the project shown here can be customized to match personalities and displaying locations.

materials

Shadow box

Sandpaper

Peach acrylic paint

Brush

Selection of decorative papers in blues, greens, pinks, and yellows

Scissors

Small pieces of cardboard

Flower and butterfly shaped punches

Rubber cement

Miniature wood fence

Clear-drying craft glue

2 small popsicle sticks

Pink embroidery floss

Decorative thread

Miniature clothespins

3 seed beads

step by step

1 Sand the shadowbox frame and wipe with a damp cloth. Allow the frame to dry, then paint it with peach acrylic paint. Allow the paint to completely dry.

2 Select several sheets of predominantly blue or green patterned paper to use for the background (sky and meadow) of your picture. Using the shadowbox inset as a template, cut a piece of blue paper and secure it to the inset with rubber cement. Cut rolling meadow shapes from the green paper and secure them to the inset with rubber cement. Cut cloud shapes and secure them to the inset with rubber cement. You may wish to glue small pieces of cardboard between cloud layers to create additional depth.

3 Remove the adhesive backing from the wood fence and position it in your picture. Create the clothesline by attaching the popsicle sticks and decorative thread with glue.

4 Cut clothing shapes freehand from remaining papers, or use the template on page xxx. Glue seed beads to your paper clothes to simulate buttons. Attach the paper clothes to the clothesline with the miniature clothespins.

5 Use the flower and butterfly punches to cut flower and butterfly shapes from remaining sheets of decorative paper. (Use colors that contrast with green and blue, such as pink and yellow.)

6 Use rubber cement to attach the butterflies and flowers to your picture. Cut small strands of embroidery thread and glue them to the butterfly shapes to finish the butterfly form.

7 Frame the collge in a shadowbox.

Designer: Megan Kirby

Artist Trading Cards

Artist Trading Cards (ATCs for short) are all the rage and a great way to acquire art. The collage techniques described below are simple—just vary the materials if you'd like to create your own unique look.

materials

Deck of playing cards

Tissue and/or origami paper

Waxed paper

Clear packing tape

Bone folder

Letters

Eyelets and eyelet setter

step by step

1 Adhere a layer of thin origami paper or tissue paper to the front and back sides of a playing card with acrylic medium. (Covering both sides will prevent warping.) Place the covered card between sheets of waxed paper, weight with a heavy book, and allow to dry overnight.

2 Choose your images as desired. Images from a fashion magazine were used here, but you can choose images from anywhere to create your desired theme. Place each image facedown on clear packing tape, then burnish with a bone folder.

3 Place the adhered image in a container of water to soften the fibers of the paper. Rub the paper backing off the tape to reveal a transparent image.

4 Cut out the transferred image as desired, then adhere it to the playing card.

5 Add a phrase to each card with a variety of lettering materials. The phrase "la mode" was used here.

6 Set an eyelet in the center top and bottom of each card. Thread ribbon, yarns, embroidery floss, or other decorative materials through the eyelets. Tie off as desired.

Designer: Terry Taylor

Designer: Diana Light

Collaged Jewelry Box

Transform plain wooden boxes into miniature treasure chests, jewelry boxes, or alternative gift packages. They're simple and inexpensive to make and a great way to showcase your favorite papers and embellishments.

materials

Wooden box

Gold acrylic paint

4 wooden beads for "feet"

Black felt

Red and gold decorative paper

Decoupage medium

Small and medium brush

All-purpose glue

Tassel

Large decorative button or bead

Small mirror

Charms and gold embellishments

step by step

1 Paint the inside edges of the box with gold paint, then paint the four wooden beads. Allow to completely dry.

2 Measure pieces of felt to fit on the inside of the box, then glue them in place.

3 Measure and cut a strip of gold paper long enough to fit around all four sides of your box top plus ⅛ inch (3 mm).

Carefully brush decoupage medium on the back side of the paper, then press in place around the box so the overlapping "seam" is in the back side of the box.

4 Measure and cut a square of gold paper to exactly fit the top of the box. Brush the back side with decoupage medium, the press in place. Allow to completely dry.

5 Cut a square of red paper slightly smaller than the top of the box. Brush the back side with decoupage medium, then carefully press in place so the gold paper background is even on all sides. Allow to completely dry.

6 Trace the circle shape from the bottom of a drinking glass onto your papers. Cut one circle from each color of paper, then cut the circles in half. Fold the half circles into fan shapes and set aside.

7 Arrange the tassel so it hangs over the front of the box, then glue the large button or bead in the top center of the box, anchoring the tassel cord in the glue under the button.

8 Insert the tips of the fans under the button and glue in place. In this design, a red fan was arranged on each side and a gold fan at the center top.

9 Glue a gold bead "foot" about ¼ inch (6 mm) in from each corner of the bottom of the box.

10 Glue the miniature mirror inside the box top, adding charms or additional embellishments if desired.

Matchbox Treasure Chests

Remember the joy you felt as a child when you hid your treasures safely away in small boxes or when you opened a beautifully wrapped tiny package? Craft stores now sell matchboxes in bulk, and their multiple surfaces just invite embellishment.

materials

2-inch-wide (5 cm) length of balsa wood

Wooden rectangle

Craft knife

Scissors

Matchboxes (available at craft supply stores)

Colored brads

Paper piercing tool

Decorative paper

Bone folder

Hot-glue gun and glue

Sheet of craft foam in color of your choice

4 paper clips in complementary color

Embellishments

step by step

1 For each box, cut a piece of balsa wood into a 2½ inch (6.5 cm) length with your craft knife.

2 Cut a piece of decorative paper slightly larger than the balsa wood. Coat the back side of the paper with a thin layer of glue, then smooth it over the top side of the balsa wood. Fold the excess paper up and around the sides of the wood as you would wrap a gift package, smoothing away any wrinkles with a bone folder.

3 Make a small vertical slit in the center front and back of the interior matchbox. Insert a brad in each hole, then open the wings and press them in place.

4 Hot glue the wrapped balsa wood to the center top of the matchbox, then hot-glue the wooden rectangle to the bottom of the matchbox.

5 Cut a piece of foam to fit the wooden bottom of the box, then hot glue in place.

6 To make feet for the box, pull the inner loop of the paper clip out toward you, then use wire cutters to trim the wire even with the larger loop.

7 Make a diagonal cut with the craft knife in each of the four corners of the foam to make room for the feet. Insert the nonlooped ends of the clips into the slits and hot glue in place, adjusting the clips so they each angle toward the outer corners of the box.

8 Decorate the top surface of your treasure boxes with your chosen embellishments. See tip below for instructions to make the vellum flowers shown on these boxes.

Designer: Suzie Millions

tip

To make your own vellum flower, stack four 1-inch strips of vellum in alternating colors. Make a hole in the center of the stacked papers and insert a small brad into the hole. Trim off the corners of the paper to form a rough circle, then snip the paper in toward the center like thin slices of pie.

Collaged Photo Mailer

Use this collaged photo mailer to display and style your panoramic photos safely and stylishly. Draw from a theme in your photo—your vacation to Italy or your child's first birthday—for inspiration. The same project can also be designed as an alternative to traditional gift wrap.

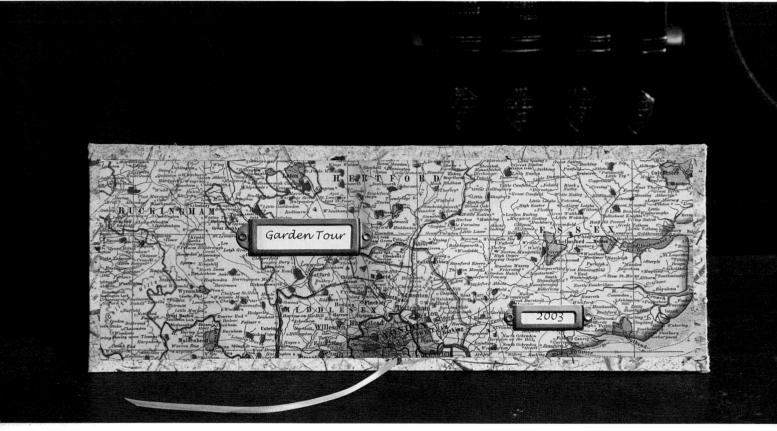

Designer: Terry Taylor

materials

Ruler

Pencil

Illustration or mat board

Craft knife

Asian paper (to use as backing)

Decorative papers (scrapbook paper, or even 'found paper' to use as theme)

Matte acrylic medium

Brush

Bone folder

Wax paper

Assorted embellishments

Photo corners

step by step

1 Measure your photos. Add ½ inch (1.3 cm) to each of the measurements so the photos will fit in the mailer comfortably. Outline the measurements on the illustration or mat board with a sharpened pencil, then cut them out with the craft knife.

2 Cut two rectangles of Asian paper slightly larger than your boards. Center each board on the paper, then trim the papers on the diagonal near the corners, cutting each paper separately.

3 Cut two rectangles of your printed paper (scrapbook paper or found paper) slightly smaller than your boards and set them aside for later. Cut two rectangles of Asian paper to the same size as your printed paper; also set them aside.

4 Brush acrylic medium on one side of your board. Lay the board on the Asian paper, acrylic side down, then smooth out any wrinkles or air pockets with the bone folder.

5 Coat the opposite side with acrylic medium, wrapping the Asian paper around the edges as neatly as possible. Place your decorative paper on this side, then repeat the process with the other board.

6 Wrap the boards in wax paper, weigh the boards with heavy books, and allow them to dry overnight.

7 While the boards dry, cut a 1-inch (2.5 cm) strip of Asian paper to the length of the boards.

8 After the boards have dried completely, you'll need to attach them together. Lay the strip of Asian paper on a piece of wax paper and brush on acrylic medium. Keep in mind that when you place the boards on the strip, your mailer needs room to close completely. For a good guide, use a scrap of your board on its edge placed

Turn the photo mailer inside out to display your photograph.

between the lengths of your boards. Press the boards flat and allow them to dry.

9 Use embellishments to decorate the cover of your mailer, attaching with acrylic medium. Inside, use photo corners to attach your photo, and voila! Now you have the perfect gift to share a special moment caught on film!

Back side of photo mailer

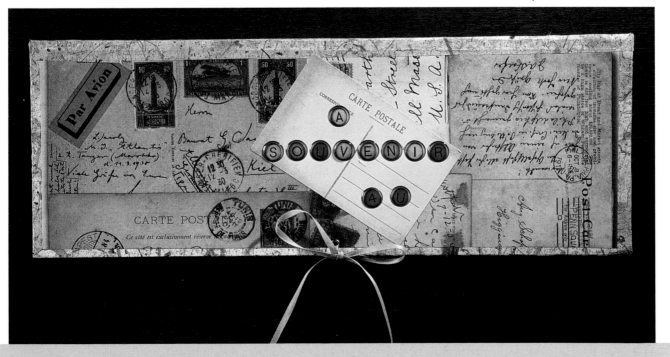

Designer: Suzie Millions

Collaged Desk Set

Undecorated paper mache forms are available in many sizes and shapes and make great bases for collage projects.

materials

Rectangular paper mache form

Decorative collage papers

Craft glue or decoupage medium

Paintbrush

Bone folder

2 wooden rectangles (cut from balsa wood or precut)

Matchbox

Paper piercing tool

Colored brad

Eyelet

Hot-glue gun and glue

Miniature basket

Small box lid (metal or carboard)

Acrylic paint

Wooden saucer bead

Cake decorating tip

Initial stickers or buttons

4 round wooden beads for "legs"

step by step

1 Cut two pieces of decorative paper, one for the top of the desk set and one for the bottom.

2 Paint the top surface with glue or decoupage medium, then place a sheet of paper over it, smoothing out any wrinkles or air pockets with a bone folder. Repeat with the bottom surface and allow the glue to completely dry.

3 Decorate the front, back and side panels of the matchbox drawer with paper, stickers, and/or stamped images.

4 Make a small vertical slit in the center front of the matchbox. Insert a brad into the hole, then open the wings to secure it in place inside the box.

5 Hot-glue a wood rectangle to the top and bottom of the match box. Decorate the top piece of wood with stamped images or stickers, then glue the matchbox onto the top left corner of the desk set.

6 Hot-glue the basket and the box lid next to the matchbox.

7 To create the pencil holder, hot-glue the saucer bead to the right side of the desk set. Glue an eyelet on top of the bead's hole, then hot-glue a cake decorating tip into the bead.

8 Personalize the desk set by adding initial letters under the pencil holder.

9 Hot-glue a wooden bead at each of the bottom four corners to serve as "legs."

This base of this collaged note paper holder was also made with purchased paper mache forms.

Collage Gallery

Above top: Encyclopedia images, magazine clippings, and decorative wrapping papers were layered over plain boxes to create decorative storage space.
Designer: Megan Kirby

Above: This miniature divider screen was crafted from foam core, then collaged with Asian papers, images, and memorabilia.
Designer: Terry Taylor

Above left: A collaged mailing envelope is a great way to surprise someone special and is sure to stand out among bills and junk mail. Be sure to use a sturdy base material that can withstand the rigors of automated mail machines.
Designer: Luann Udell

Left: The cover and interior pages of an old book provide multiple collage surfaces. The designer of this book included fibers, glitter, stickers, and specialty papers on her pages.
Designer: Kathy Anderson

Above: Virtually any surface becomes a canvas to create collaged images. These bottles were covered with layers of specialty papers in a variety of shapes.
Designer: Terry Taylor

Right: Collage a picture-perfect frame for your favorite gardener with printed tissue papers and miniature garden embellishments.
Designer: Allison Smith

Above: Layers of patterned tissue paper and acrylic paints transformed plain wooden trays into contemporary showpieces.
Designer: Terry Taylor

Right: Any material is fair game for a collage crafter! Here, a collection of seed packages, specialty papers printed with bird images, and stamps were collaged on a wooden birdhouse base.
Designer: Diane Peterson

Paper Cutting, Punching & Piercing

What better way to indulge your whimsical side than by playing with paper cutting, punching, and piercing? The techniques are incredibly simple, and the results can be spectacular, letting you dress up everything from scrapbooking pages to handcrafted cards to gift bags.

Save Those Scraps!

Trimmings from decorative-edged scissors and decorative paper punches may look like trash, but a good collection of them can be a crafter's best friend.

Make at least a few passes with your decorative-edged scissors and a few cutouts with your favorite punches every time you have left-over scraps of decorative paper from card making or other paper projects — your collection will grow in no time!

Organize your cutouts and paper strips in a small plastic box with compartments. Sort them by color and pattern.

Use decorative scissor strips as borders for cards and scrapbooking, or mix and match them in your next collage project.

Use paper punch shapes as corner frames for photos or as decorative accents.

Embellish paper cutouts with beads or embroidery.

Whoops — made a crafting mistake? Cover it with a paper cutout or decorative strip and only you will know.

materials

decorative punches

Punches can be found in dozens of patterns and several styles. Look for press punches, squeeze punches, and edge punches.

decorative-edged scissors

Remember when borrowing your mom's pinking sheers from her sewing box was the only way to get a decorative edge on paper? Thankfully, those days are gone, and a fun variety of patterns are available today, many of them so inexpensive that you'll want them all!

paper piercing tool

This simple tool — sometimes referred to as an awl — lets you press small holes in very precise locations. Crafting tool kits often come with piercing tools that have piercing tips of different sizes, giving you maximum flexibility.

paper

Light- and medium-weight papers are ideal for paper cutting and punching, while medium- and heavy-weight papers are ideal for piercing. If you fall in love with a paper whose weight isn't ideal, though, try working with it anyway. You never know what creative solution you might come up with.

cardboard or foam core

Cardboard and foam core scraps are great for protecting work surfaces. After all, you really don't want a pierced-paper design permanently engraved into your dining room table, do you?

basic techniques

cutting paper

Decorative-edged scissors have created a world of creative opportunity for crafters. For good results, use long, smooth motions to cut your paper. For perfect corners and pattern matches, you may need to make several practice cuts to get just the look you want.

basic techniques

punching paper

Craft manufacturers have come a long way since the days of the simple hole punch, and today's punches are fun and easy to use.

1 To use a press punch, insert the paper in the punch, carefully aligning the punch pattern on your paper. Press down gently but firmly — voila!

2 To use a squeeze punch, insert the paper in the punch, aligning the punch pattern as directed above, and squeeze.

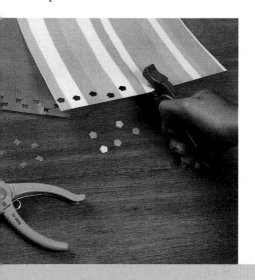

3 To punch thin papers such as tissue paper, you may need to add bulk to get clean edges on your punched shapes. To add bulk, simply place a sheet of medium-weight paper behind the tissue paper. Layering multiple sheets of tissue paper often works as well, depending on the sharpness of your punch.

paper piercing

Paper piercing is a great way to add decorative touches to just about any type of paper. Quilt books are good sources for patterns, or you can trace basic shapes from a multitude of sources.

1 To create a pierced design, enlarge or reduce a pattern to a suitable size. Tape the paper you want to pierce on top of a piece of cardboard, then tape the pattern over it with its right side facing up.

2 Following the outline of the pattern, insert your paper piercing tool straight down and remove it the same way. Work your way around the pattern, taking care to keep the distances between the pierce marks fairly even.

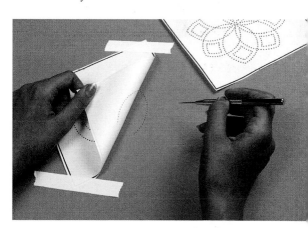

3 Remove the pattern from your paper and the paper from the cardboard.

Corrugated Photo Frame

Today's corrugated craft papers come in a bright array of fabulous colors. The paper is sturdy enough to be used in a variety of crafts, from card making to frame making.

materials

Corrugated cardboard

Mat board or heavy cardboard

Craft knife

Craft glue

Binder clips

Fancy paper clips

Glass beads

This frame is also a great way to display special postcards. Now your favorite museum paintings and vacation sights can become part of your home decor!

step by step

1 Using the craft knife, cut two rectangles of equal dimensions: one from the corrugated cardboard and the other from the mat board.

2 Measure and mark a window on the middle of your cut corrugated rectangle slightly smaller than the dimensions of the photograph you want to frame. Cut out the shape with the craft knife.

3 Cut a right-angle triangle shape out of matt board with the craft knife, then use the knife to score a seam along the vertical leg of the triangle.

4 Fold along the scored seam and glue the fold to the back of the mat board. Use binder clips to secure the pieces in place as they dry.

5 Apply a line of glue along the bottom front side of the mat board, and affix the bottom of the corrugated cardboard rectangle along this edge. Use paper clips to secure the pieces in place as they dry. (Note: Binder clips will crush the corrugated cardboard.)

6 Open and straighten the outside edge of the paper clips. Slide several beads on and bend the clip back into place.

7 Tape your photo on the mat board and use your beaded paper clips to hold the top edge of the frame in place

Designer: Kathryn Temple

Embellished Gift Bag

If you're a scrapbooker or card maker, no doubt you have a fine collection of embellishments you just couldn't resist, plus a fair amount of paper scraps. Put those two materials together and you can create unique gift bags in minutes.

materials

Decorative paper

Decorative-edged scissors

Clear-drying craft glue

Scrapbooking trims and embellishments

Tissue paper

step by step

1 Cut a piece of decorative paper using decorative-edged sciessors about 1½ inches (7.5 cm) smaller than the front of your gift bag. Add a light layer of glue to the back side, and smooth it in place on the front side of the bag.

2 Cut a second piece of contrasting decorative paper ¼ to ½ inch (6 to 12 mm) smaller than the first piece. Add a light layer of glue to the back side, and smooth in place on top of the first paper, centering carefully.

3 Arrange your favorite scrapbooking trims and embellishments on the second sheet of paper — colorful hearts were used in this project — and adhere in place.

4 Add a few dots of glue in the bottom corners of the gift bag. Fluff a piece or two of colored tissue paper and line the inside of the gift bag with it.

Designer: Susan McBride

tip *While your creative energy is brimming and your supplies are out, why not make matching gift tags or small note cards?*

Paisley Power

Here's a playful picture frame that will add a note of cheer to any room. Try varying the colors and motif to create custom designs for any room or for special gifts.

materials

Unfinished wooden frame

Acrylic paint

Tissue paper (two colors)

Stapler

Paisley template

Pencil

Decorative-edged scissors

Decorative hole punches

Foam brush

Decoupage medium

Designer: Terry Taylor

step by step

1 Paint the frame with two coats of acrylic paint following the manufacturer's directions. Let it dry overnight.

2 Photocopy and enlarge or reduce the paisley template as desired. Cut out the paisley shape.

3 Keep your tissue paper folded. Lay the paisley template on the tissue and trace around the shape with a pencil.

4 To cut multiple paisley shapes at once, staple about $\frac{1}{2}$ inch (13 mm) from around the outside of the pencil marks.

5 Cut out the paisley shape with the decorative-edged scissors. Keep the stack of tissue together as you make the last cut.

6 Use the hole punches to create decorative patterns in the paisley shapes.

7 Use a large decorative punch to punch out some larger shapes (flowers, dots, or any other shape).

8 Spread a coat of decoupage medium on a small area of the frame. Lay one tissue paisley on the frame. Use your foam brush to pat the shape into place. Gently brush the shape to remove any air bubbles or wrinkles. Be careful, the wet tissue will tear easily!

9 Cover the surface of the box with tissue shapes. Allow the frame to dry overnight, then give the frame a final coat of decoupage medium to seal the tissue shapes.

Paper Perfect Luminaries

Remember making craft projects in elementary school with plain brown lunch bags? Lunch bags are still great for crafting, but now they're made in a surprising range of fun colors. These paper bag luminaries are just one of the many possibilities.

materials

Lunch bags

Flower and leaf paper punches

2 sheets of colorful,
   contrasting paper

Decorative-edged scissors

Glue

Votive candle in candle holder

Sand

step by step

1 With the bag folded, carefully punch two flowers in the center front of the bag. Allow the punch to go through the back of the bag, also.

2 Cut a rectangle from one of the decorative papers to fit inside the back side of the bag, then glue in place. (This step will allow the paper's color and pattern to show through the punched flower holes on the front of the bag.)

3 Cut two strips with the decorative-edged scissors to fit the front side of the bag, one narrow and one wide, from the second sheet of paper. Glue them in place, smoothing out any air bubbles with your fingertips.

4 Cut two flowers with the flower punch from the second paper, and glue them over the holes on the back side of the bag.

5 Punch four leaf shapes from a lunch bag, and glue in place under the flowers.

6 Fill the bottom of each luminary with an inch or two (2.5 to 5 cm) of sand, then press the votive candle securely into the sand.

NOTE: Never leave a burning candle unattended, especially in paper luminary bags.

Designer: Megan Kirby

Quotable Magnets

A well-turned phrase can fire the imagination—which is what makes quotations printed on vellum such fun! Just pick a saying that speaks to you; then create a magnet to match. Who knows? Even your boss's latest memo might seem more inspiring if it's affixed to your filing cabinet with a magnet bearing just the right words...

materials

Vellum printed with quotations

Variety of novelty papers

Sheet of adhesive-backed magnet

Double-sided tape

Clear-drying craft glue

Opaque craft paint

Decoupage medium, matte finish

Seed beads

Nylon thread

Yarn

Scissors

Craft knife

Paintbrushes

Needle

Lamination/sticker machine with an adhesive cartridge, or a glue stick

Decorative-edged scissors

Embossing tool (optional)

step by step

1 While you'll almost certainly want to choose a quotation and design your magnet to suit, the following steps describe how to achieve the specific effects featured in the projects shown in the photo. In every case, though, start by choosing a quotation and cutting it out: The quotation's length and orientation will suggest the shape to cut it to. The shape and size of the quotation will dictate the shape and size of the other pieces of paper you use.

2 To make a project similar to the green rectangular magnet bearing the William Shakespeare quotation, you'll need two rectangles of decorative paper, one slightly larger than the other. Cut the smaller rectangle from paper embossed with at least three different elements, saving the scraps for the next step. Cut the larger rectangle from another paper in a complementary color. For the project shown, the designer chose a pale green paper embossed with birds and flowers (to echo the daffodil and sparrow mentioned in the quotation), as well as a roughly clover-shaped form. For the second sheet, she chose a pale blue paper.

3 Choose one of the elements from the embossed paper to use at the top and the bottom of the quotation. Carefully cut two of that element from the paper scraps, using your craft knife. For the project shown, the designer selected the clover shape. After cutting out the clovers, she painted their edges very pale green.

4 Cut one each of the other two elements from the

embossed paper—in the project shown, the bird and flower. After cutting them out, the designer painted the flower yellow and the bird blue. When the paint was dry, she stitched a green seed bead to the center of the flower. After you've painted, stitched, or otherwise embellished your cutouts, glue each one to one of the cutouts from Step 3. Then allow the glue to dry.

5 Now, assemble the magnet: Apply glue to the back of the cutouts you completed in Step 4, and use them as "stickers" to attach the vellum quotation to the rectangle of embossed paper. Then glue the embossed paper rectangle to the larger rectangle. Trim the edges of the larger rectangle with decorative-edged scissors. Finally, cut a rectangle of adhesive-backed magnet and attach it the back of the larger rectangle.

(continues on following page)

6 To create a project similar to the blue magnet, start by cutting the vellum quotation into the shape of a row of houses. Cut a slightly smaller row of houses from a sheet of pale blue decorative paper; then cut the row into separate houses. Make win-dows for the houses by cutting small squares of yellow paper in various sizes.

7 As you can see from the photo, the houses will be mounted to a rectangle of dark blue paper, which is mounted on a slightly larger rectangle of turquoise paper that's flecked with silver glitter. Cut these rectangles.

8 Glue the pale blue paper houses to the smaller rectangle from Step 7, using the project photo as a guide. Attach the yellow windows on top of the paper houses, using decoupage medium. Apply adhesive to the back of the row of vellum houses, using your lamination/sticker machine. (Alternatively, you can attach the vellum with your glue stick.) Then press the row of vellum houses in place over the paper houses.

9 In the project shown, the designer used an embossing tool to emboss the vellum slightly. She also added "snowflakes" over the houses by stitching clear white seed beads to the dark blue paper. Embellish the houses and the sky overhead as desired; then glue them to the large rectangle of turquoise paper. Cut a rectangle of adhesive-backed magnet to size and attach it to the back of the turquoise paper.

10 To make the butterfly magnet, you'll need three different decorative papers: a yellow patterned paper for the background and two different pink, patterned papers for the wings. You can use either one of the pink papers or any other paper you like for the butterfly's body.

11 Freehand draw the upper and lower wings of the butterfly body, or trace

around the photo on page 217. Trace the templates on to your papers. Cut out the wings and body; then, from each pink paper, cut two circles for the decorative spots. If desired, paint the edges and centers of the decorative spots with pale green and yellow paint, using the project photo as a guide. Attach the spots to the wings with decoupage medium.

12 Cut a rectangle from the yellow patterned paper; then attach the wings to the background rectangle with double-sided tape.

13 Wrap the butterfly's body with decorative yarn, using glue to secure it; then attach the body in place between the wings, using either glue or double-sided tape. Use either a paintbrush or a marker to draw the butterfly's antennae directly on the yellow background paper.

14 Apply adhesive to the back of the vellum quotation with the lamination/sticker machine; then press it into place over the butterfly.

15 Cut a rectangle of adhesive-backed magnet to size and mount it to the back of the yellow background rectangle.

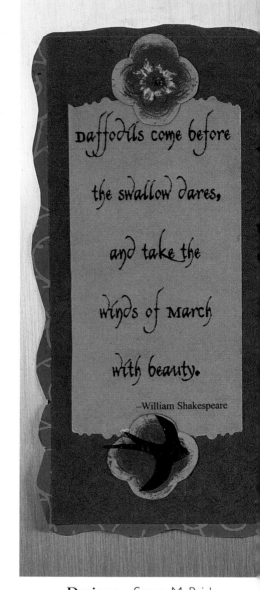

Daffodils come before the swallow dares, and take the winds of March with beauty.

–William Shakespeare

Designer: Susan McBride

Paper-Punched Lamp Shade

Handmade lamp shades are easy to make and a great way to add designer touches to your home. Create interesting patterns by punching your own designs in the paper, or follow the outlines of an embossed or printed paper.

materials

6-inch-diameter (15 cm) lamp shade frame and hardware*

1 piece of medium-gauge hardware cloth, measuring 7 x 12 inches (18 x 30.5 cm)

28-gauge wire

2 sheets of re, embossed paper, each measuring 12 x 12 inches (30.5 x 30.5 cm)

Clear-drying raft glue

Black PVC craft lace

Black beaded fringe

Wire cutters

Scissors or craft knife

Ruler

Pencil

Hole-punch tool with ⅛-inch (3mm) and ³⁄₁₆-inch heads (5mm)

Hammer

Self-healing cutting mat

Clothespin (optional)

tip

If you have trouble finding a new lamp shade frame and associated hardware, look for an old cloth or paper lamp shade at yard sales and flea markets. Then, just cut away the unwanted paper or fabric and keep the frame and hardware.

step by step

1 Start by making a form to build your lamp shade around. You'll remove the form later—it won't be part of the finished project—so it doesn't have to be perfect or even pretty. Simply roll the hardware cloth around the lamp shade frame to create a long 6-inch-diameter (15 cm) cylinder. Overlap the hardware cloth's edges, cut a length of wire several feet (1 m) long, and use it to "sew" the cylinder, stitching along the length of the seam formed by the cloth's overlap. Attach the lampshade frame to the cylinder with a few whipstitches around the wire rim of the frame at the top of the cylinder.

2 You'll need one large sheet of paper measuring 9 x 20 inches (23 x 51 cm) to cover the form and create the shade. Clever crafter that you are, you've already noticed that the materials list calls for two 12-inch squares of paper. To make the large 9- x-20-inch sheet, cut a 2-inch (5 cm) strip from one side of each square, and a 3-inch (7.5 cm) strip from an adjoining side to make two 9- x-10-inch (23 x 25 cm) rectangles. Trim two of the strips you just cut to ½ inch (1.3 cm) wide and 9 inches long.

3 Arrange the two 9- x-10-inch rectangles side by side, with their 9-inch edges touching, but

(continues on following page)

not overlapping, and the 10-inch edges even. Apply a thin layer of glue to one side of one of the ½-inch-wide strips from Step 2, and place it over the 9-inch-long seam between the two rectangles, tacking the pieces together. Now, you have a single sheet of 9- x 20-inch (23 x 51 cm) paper. The side with the strip is the back of the sheet. Save the other strip for Steps 8 and 9. Allow the glue to dry.

4 As you can see from the photo, the red paper is stitched to the rim of the lamp shade frame with black PVC lace. Although you won't make these stitches until Step 11, mark the holes for them now: Measure ½ inch down from the top 20-inch edge of the paper and use a pencil to make light marks spaced ½ inch apart along the entire length of the paper.

5 Choose a hole-punch pattern (or follow an embossed design), and mark the holes. Leave the bottom ½-inch border of the shade unpunched, though, so your beaded fringe will lay flat.

6 Place the marked paper on your cutting mat. Using the hole-punch tool and a ⅛-inch (3 mm) head, punch the holes for the black PVC lace, and for about two of every three holes you marked in Step 5. Then change to a ³/16-inch (5 mm) head and punch the remaining holes.

7 Cut a length of beaded fringe about ½-inch longer than the circumference of the lamp shade frame. Apply glue along the bottom border of the front of the sheet of paper and press the fringe into place. Allow the glue to dry. You'll use the extra bit of fringe that hangs beyond the paper's edges to overlap after you assemble the shade.

8 Turn the sheet of paper over, laying it face down on your work surface. Apply a line of glue right along one of the sheet's 9-inch edges. Glue the ½-inch-wide strip along this edge so that half the strip's width hangs beyond the edge; you'll apply glue to this overlap and use it to tack the ends of the sheet together. Allow the glue to dry.

9 Roll the paper around the cylinder. Apply glue along the length of the portion of the tacking strip that shows, and press the edge of the paper sheet in place along it. The tacking strip should be completely hidden now. Hold the seam together until the glue dries or secure it with a clothespin. Glue the overlapping edges of the beaded fringe together to make a neat seam.

10 To remove the form from your lamp shade, start by snipping away the whipstitches holding the hardware cloth to the frame's rim. Then carefully pull the hardware cloth frame out of the paper.

11 Set the frame's rim back inside the top of the paper lamp shade. Attach the lamp shade to the rim with the black craft lace, whipstitching through the holes you made in Step 6.

12 Add the lamp shade to your favorite low-wattage lamp, flip the switch, and enjoy.

Designers: Diana Light & Torin Dilley

Fabulous Faux Mosaic Tray

Who needs the fuss and mess of ceramic tile and grout when in just a couple of hours you can "tile" a great tray like this for tonight's party?

materials

Unpainted wooden tray

Sandpaper

Clean cloth

Matte latex paint, white

Paper in two or three solid colors

Glue (optional)

Piece of glass, cut to fit the serving tray

Paintbrushes

Scissors

Square decorative paper punch

Leaf decorative paper punch

Lamination/sticker machine with an adhesive cartridge (optional)

tip *You can also contrast a solid paper mosaic project by adding printed papers; just be sure to limit your color and pattern selection so the design doesn't get too busy.*

step by step

1 Sand the tray smooth, then wipe away the dust with a clean, damp cloth. Allow the tray to air dry for a few minutes before painting it white. You may need to apply several coats of paint for complete coverage; if so, allow each coat to dry before sanding it lightly and applying the next coat.

2 Cut the paper into widths that will fit your lamination/sticker machine; then, following the manufacturer's instructions, run the paper through the machine to apply adhesive. (Alternatively, you can "lay" the tiles using regular craft glue; just wait until you're ready to start adhering them in place before applying the glue.)

3 Next, use decorative paper punches to create your tiles from the adhesive-backed paper. For the project shown, use a simple square punch and a leaf-shaped punch.

4 Before sticking the tiles in place, take some time to lay out your design, using a ruler to ensure an even grid. When you're satisfied with your layout, you may find it useful to indicate the placement of the tiles with very light pencil marks.

5 Adhere the square tiles in place, working on one row at a time. If you're using glue, avoid bubbling and wrinkles by applying the glue to the back of each tile as you go, using a small paintbrush to ensure a thin, even layer.

6 After you've laid all the square tiles, snip the leaf-shaped tiles in half. Using the project photo as a guide, carefully adhere the half-leaf tiles.

7 Slip the sheet of glass in place over the mosaic; then load up the tray with hors d'oeuvres!

Designer: Terry Taylor

Luminous Vellum Flower Garland

There's no doubt about it: Even a plain strand of little white lights instantly livens up a room. Add these easy-to-make vellum flowers to that strand, and the result is nothing short of sheer, luminous enchantment.

materials

Sheets of vellum in various colors and patterns

Templates on pages 308 and 309

Strand of white lights

Scissors

Pencil

Hole punch

Flat-edged tool such as a putty knife

step by step

1 Start by turning to pages 308 and 309 where you'll find templates for cutting the flowers. As you can see, the templates vary in size. Depending on which template you're using, you'll need a 2-, 3-, or 4-inch (5 cm, 7.5 cm, or 10 cm) square of vellum to create it.

2 Determine how many squares of each size you'll need and cut them from your vellum paper.

3 Fold the squares of vellum into quadrants, using the particular template you're work-ing with as a guide. Note that some of the templates require that the folds be made across the square's horizontal midline, while others require that the folds be made across the square's diagonal midline.

4 Unfold a paper square and place it on top of your template. Using a pencil, lightly trace the template design onto the square.

5 Refold the paper and cut out the design. Then unfold the paper and make a hole at the flower piece's center with the hole punch. Your hole punch may not reach all the way to the middle of the larger pieces; if that's the case, simply fold the piece in half and punch a half hole centered on the fold-ed edge. Repeat to trace and cut your remaining template pieces.

6 Now, "affix" the flowers to the light strand. The flow-ers are actually held in place by the light bulbs, so to install a flower, start by carefully loosen-ing a bulb from its socket, using a flat-edged tool such as a putty knife. Although it should go without saying that the light strand absolutely must be unplugged for this step, we'll say it anyway: Make sure the light strand is unplugged for this step!

7 Slip the vellum template pieces over the end of the bulb, sliding them down to near the bulb's bottom end. Then reinsert the bulb into its socket so that the paper pieces are sand-wiched between. Repeat until the entire light strand is flowered.

NOTE: Always unplug the light garland when you leave the room.

Designer: Kathryn Temple

Pleated Photo Border

Paper crafters are always searching for new, fun ways to frame their favorite photographs. This project combines paper cutting, piercing, and folding to create a unique look.

materials

Original photograph or color copy

2 sheets of ivory or white vellum

Medium-weight white paper

Metallic paper in a dark color that complements your photograph

Adhesive mounting squares

Scissors

Clear-drying craft glue

Narrow ribbon

Decorative-edged scissors

Paper piercing tool

Cardboard or self-healing mat

Bone folder

Gift tag and chain

Sticker letters

Designer: Beth Berutich

step by step

1 Mount your photograph on the ivory or white vellum, then trim the paper's edges to ½ inch (12 mm) on all sides.

2 Frame the photograph on all sides with narrow ribbon, securing with small amounts of glue and mitering the corners.

3 Trace the outline of the bordered photograph onto the back side of the white paper. Add ¼ inch (6 mm) on all sides, then cut out the paper with the decorative-edged scissors.

4 Place the paper you just cut on a piece of cardboard or self-healing mat, then pierce holes in the paper to complement the pattern made by your decorative-edged scissors.

5 To make your pierced holes more visible, place the metallic paper behind your framed photograph, then trim it just enough so it shows through the pierced holes.

6 Cut four strips of white paper that are ¾-inch (18 mm) wide and four times longer than the four sides of the photo.

7 Pleat the paper strips by folding the paper back onto itself. You may choose to space your pleats any distance you find pleasing. Flatten the pleated strips with the bone folder.

8 Trace the outline of your bordered photograph onto the back side of a sheet of vellum and add ½ inch to all sides. Cut out the paper with regular scissors.

9 Glue the pleated strips to the vellum you cut in Step 8, starting at the top and bottom edges and then working down the sides. Trim off any excess paper.

10 Decorate one corner of the photograph by attaching a bow with ribbon streamers and a name tag

Photo Cards

With color copiers it's easy to create dozens of personalized cards for baby, engagement, and moving announcements, as well as for Christmas holidays. The multiple paper borders are a great way to use up leftover scraps.

Designer: Megan Kirby

materials

Card stock

3 patterns of decorative paper

3 pairs of decorative-edged scissors, each in a different pattern

Bone folder

Clear-drying craft glue

Flower paper punch

step by step

1 Cut the card stock into a long rectangle that's the height you want your finished card to be and twice the width. Fold in half and smooth the crease with a bonefolder.

2 Make a color photocopy of the photo you want to showcase, enlarging or reducing as needed so it will be approximately an inch (2.5 cm) smaller on all sides than the front of your card.

3 Trim the photocopy, then mount it in the center of one of your decorative papers. Trim the edges of the paper with decorative-edged scissors, allowing a narrow border.

4 Mount the bordered photocopy from Step 3 onto another decorative paper. Trim the edges with a narrow border with a different edging pattern.

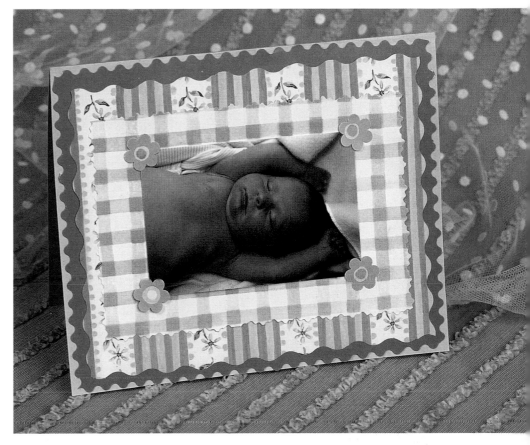

5 Repeat Step 4 with the third decorative paper and another edging pattern, then mount the multiple-bordered photograph on the center front of the card.

6 Punch flower shapes from one of the decorative papers and glue them in the corners of the photo.

Let your photo inspire your choices of paper colors and patterns, and no two cards will ever be the same.

tip

When possible, take advantage of designs of the paper you're punching. In this project, the punches were positioned so the flower centers in the punch lined up with the polka dots in the paper to create flower centers.

Designer: Marthe Le Van

Pieced Paper Quilt

Why should fabric crafters have all the fun? The patchwork patterns of many traditional quilts can be easily replicated in paper using combinations of squares and/or triangles. Add faux "stitching" lines if you like with puff paint or markers.

materials

Sheet of foam core in color of
your choice

1 sheet each of 8 decorative
papers

Decoupage medium, matte or gloss

Straightedge or large ruler

Pencil

Paper cutter

Plastic container lid

Small foam paintbrush

Large foam paintbrush

step by step

1 Draw a straight line an inch (2.5 cm) down from the top of one of the long sides of the right side of your foam core.

2 Use the paper cutter to cut the decorative papers into ¾-inch (18 mm) squares. Separate the squares by pattern into eight piles.

3 Experiment with placing different colors and patterns next to each other, referring to the illustration on page 316 and the project photo as a guide. Assign each pile of squares an A through H letter from the illustration.

4 Pour a bit of decoupage medium into the plastic container lid. Beginning about an inch in from the top left side of the foam core, brush a thin, even coat of decoupage medium

on the center back of an A square. Gently place the square in place.

5 Referring to the illustration, continue working your way across the top row, adding one square at a time in the correct paper. Note: Your design will not begin to appear until you have applied several rows of squares.

6 Continue adding rows of paper squares, following the pattern in the illustration until you finish the quilt.

7 Use the large foam paintbrush to apply a topcoat of decoupage medium over the entire quilt. Allow to completely dry. Frame the quilt before hanging if desired, or simply trim off the excess foam core, leaving just enough to create a decorative border.

Sparkling Star Ornaments

These distinctive tree ornaments are simple enough to make so you can easily cover an entire tree or create a good-sized stash of last-minute holiday gifts. Vary the card stock and bead colors to match existing ornaments.

materials

White card stock

Star template (page 305)

Ruler and pencil

Hole punch tool with ¹⁄₁₆- and ⅛-inch (1.5 and 3 mm) heads (an awl or large needle can be used instead)

Self-healing mat or corrugated cardboard

Hammer

Craft knife

Gold headpins (2 per ornament)

Gold jump rings (2 per ornament)

Beads

Small chain-nose pliers

Small round-tip pliers

Wire cutters

tip

When opening and closing jump rings, never pull them 'apart', as it weakens the metal. Instead, move one side of the ring forward and one backward to create a gap.

step by step

1 Cut the template into three separate stars. Discard the smallest.

2 Trace inside and outside the largest star onto the card stock with a sharpened pencil. Place the smaller star in the center and trace it inside. When you are finished, your drawing should look like the template. Be sure to leave breaks in the lines at the top and bottom of the interior stars to remind you where the cutting lines should stop.

3 Use your pencil to make dots where you want your hole punches, then make your holes with the hole punch, awl, or needle, protecting your work surface with a self-healing mat or a piece of corrugated cardboard if necessary. Punch a larger hole at the top and bottom of the star for hanging.

4 Using the ruler as a guide, cut out the star with your craft knife, starting with the interior and moving to the outside. Be sure not to cut through the tops and bottoms of the middle and smallest stars.

5 To create the dangle, slide a bead onto a headpin. Grasp the headpin about ⅞ inch (about 2 cm) from the opposite end with small round-tip pliers. Bend the headpin 90 degrees, then use your other hand to bend the headpin up and around the tips of the pliers to form a loop.

6 Holding the top of the loop with the round tip pliers with your left hand (assuming you're right handed), use the chain-nose pliers in your right hand to grasp the end of the loop, wrapping the pin around the straight part of itself several times. Trim the end of the pin with the wire cutter.

Designer: Diana Light

7 Insert the jump ring through the base of the star and connect the dangle.

8 To create the hanger, cut the head off the headpin, then repeat Step 6. Use the round-tip pliers to bend the pin into a hook about halfway, so that it resembles an earring hook, then connect the jump ring to the top of the star and connect the hook.

9 For a three-dimensional effect, fold each interior star in the opposite direction, taking care not to tear through the connecting areas of paper. Fold them back for flat storage.

Paper Sculpture Angels

Ah, Christmas. Everyone likes to decorate, but who has the time? Add this easy but elegant accent to your Christmas decor. Use these angels as centerpieces, tree toppers, or place markers. You can also make miniature versions for gift tags and tree ornaments.

materials

Medium- to heavy-weight paper
Stapler
Craft knife
Scissors
Decorative punches
Decorative-edged scissors
Clear-drying craft glue

Designer: Terry Taylor

step by step

1 Make several photo-copies of the template on page 304. Do not cut out the pattern.

2 Staple a photocopied template to your paper on the outside of the angel.

3 On a flat cutting surface, use a craft knife and cut the interior cuts first; use scissors to cut out the rest of the template.

4 Use decorative punches and decorative-edged scissors to add personal touches to the skirt hem, halo, and wings.

5 Bring the skirt together at the back and glue the two edges together.

6 Glue the hands together. To make the hands appear higher, glue the backs of the hands together. To make the arms more full from the body, glue the fronts of the hands together. Allow to completely dry before moving.

7 Contour the wings to the desired shape.

tip *Wan't a little more holiday sparkle? These angels are easily embellished with glitter and paint. Try giving each angel a gold halo, or light them from within with party lights.*

Marvelous Mock Stained Glass

If you've always loved the look of stained glass, but weren't quite sure about having to cut glass and weld metal (it just sounds scary, doesn't it?), this is the perfect project for you. Gorgeously translucent and available in endless colors and patterns, vellum and tissue papers mimic stained glass beautifully. And all you'll need to work with them are plain old scissors and a glue stick.

materials

Black cardboard or poster board

Tissue paper in a variety of colors

Vellum in metallic colors

Glue stick

Photocopier

Pencil

Craft knife

Scissors

step by step

1 Start by enlarging one of the templates on pages 310 and 311 (or a favorite personal design) to the desired size, using a photocopier. Then trace the template onto the back of the black cardboard or poster board.

2 Using your craft knife, carefully cut out the design you just traced. You may find it easier to cut the design's interior-most windows first and work your way outward. This way, you'll decrease the chances of tearing the delicate bridges (the pieces of cardboard that remain after the windows have been cut).

3 Next, cut the "glass" windows. Simply trim pieces of either vellum or tissue paper to roughly the same shape as the windows they're to fill, but sized just a little larger.

4 Working on the back side of the cardboard, apply a thin coat of glue to the window bridges; then smooth the paper pieces into place and allow the glue to dry. Display your panel as desired.

Designer: Kathryn Temple

Pierced Paper Scrapbooking Page

Scrapbookers are always searching for creative ways to coordinate images in their photographs with their page designs, and pierced paper patterns are a fun design option. The same technique can be used to create frames for headlines or photos.

materials

Background paper

Tape

Paper piercing tool

Piece of cardboard or self-healing mat

2 sheets of black paper

Sheet of white paper

4 sheets of contrasting decorative paper

Adhesive mounting squares

Banner template

Photo mounting squares

Clear-drying craft glue

Sticker letters in two sizes

French curve

step by step

1 Enlarge the template below to the desired size. Tape your background paper to the cardboard or the self-healing mat, then tape your design on top of the paper.

2 Carefully pierce over the pattern template in straight up and down motions. Remove the tape from the pattern.

3 Mount your photo with multiple borders, then mount the bordered photo in the center of your butterfly.

4 Create a banner for the text. Make a slightly larger banner in a contrasting color for a border and glue them together.

5 Add a headline with sticker letters in the banner, then attach the banner to the background paper.

6 Mount the background paper of your page to a piece of black paper to enhance the pierced paper effect.

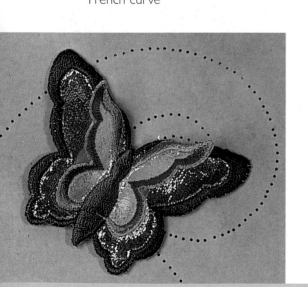

Designer: Beth Berutich

Paper Cutting, Punching & Piercing Gallery

Right: Pop-up cards are always a hit, and this one features red hearts and ribbon for a Valentine memento. Designer: Annie Cicale

Below left: Transform a blank card into a work of art with easy, creative paper punching . Designer: Terry Taylor

Below right: Would you love to send intricate, papercut greeting cards to everyone on your list but don't want to invest hundreds of hours? Just make color copies of your favorite papercut design onto blank card forms, enlarging or reducing the design to fit the card. Designer: Deborah Carter

Right: Simple paper punched circles create a twinkling star effect in this nine-pointed paper star light. Designer: Anne Ashley

Bottom right: Remember the black on white portrait silhouettes your grade school teacher helped you make? The realistic effect of these contemporary versions is created by outlining a pet's head shape from a copy of a photograph, then using that shape as a template. Designer: Terry Taylor

Below left: Don't throw those paper scraps away! The front of a card is the perfect place to create faux mosaics — customize the image to the recipient. Designer: Margaret Desmond Dahm

Below: Handmade papers torn against a ruler to create a rough edge mimic the classic look of unglazed ceramic mosaics. Designer: Terry Taylor

241

Paper Quilling, Rolling & Weaving

The designers contributing projects to this chapter have updated the traditional crafts of paper weaving and quilling, creating exquisite paper treasures with a contemporary look. Card makers, scrapbookers, and gift givers will quickly recognize the potential for weaving and quilling to add novel design touches to their work.

materials

paper strips

The first item on your shopping list should be paper. Quilled and woven designs can be created from a variety of paper stocks — just avoid papers that are extremely thin or extremely thick. You can purchase packages of precut paper strips and save yourself some time, or just cut your own.

paper cutter

If you choose to cut your own paper strips, a personal paper cutter will be one of the best purchases you ever make. Miniature cutters are now available, so you don't have to make room for another large piece of equipment.

twirling tool

Although this sounds like a specific tool, you can actually use a variety of household items to create varied effects. An embroidery needle or hat pin works well for tighter coils, while a wooden cooking skewer works well for looser coils.

adhesive

Any liquid, clear-dry craft glue will give good results.

toothpicks

Inexpensive wood or plastic toothpicks provide an easy way to apply small dabs of glue to quilled shapes.

removable tape

Paper weaving projects will go more smoothly and the end project will be much neater if you use a small amount of tape to secure the weaving to a flat surface while it's in progress.

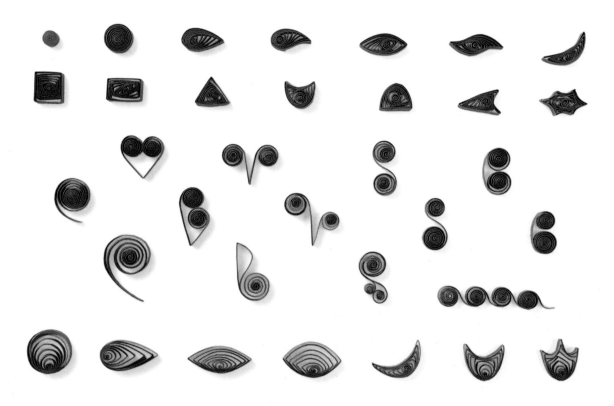

basic techniques

quilling paper

Quilled paper projects usually involve two distinct stages: making paper coils, then assembling the individual coils into an interesting design or pattern. To create the design or pattern, refer to the specific instructions that accompany each project.

1 Roll each length of paper around your chosen twirling tool, beginning at one end of the strip and rolling tightly to the end.

3 Apply glue to the ends of the strips at their sides with a toothpick to secure your quilled shape.

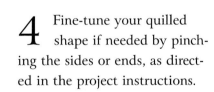

2 Lay the tool on a flat surface and allow the tension of circles to release the desired amount.

4 Fine-tune your quilled shape if needed by pinching the sides or ends, as directed in the project instructions.

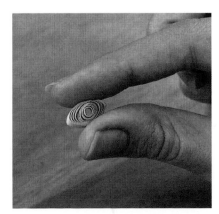

basic techniques

Attention Scrapbookers!

Always looking for unique ways to border your photos and add pizzazz to your background papers? Crimped and woven papers will offer you a world of new possibilities.

For photo backgrounds, crimp delicate papers to add sturdiness or medium-weight papers to create corrugated cardboard effects.

For background papers, weave a background of assorted papers, adding lengths of ribbon and/or decorative fibers.

Make your own crimped bows and ribbon streamers by running a length of lightweight paper through your crimping machine. Cut the crimped paper into shorter lengths and form two loops for the bows, then attach ribbon streamers under them. Add a small silk flower or scrapbooking embellishment in the center of the bow.

crimping paper

Crimping adds intriguing texture to even the plainest of papers. The technique is simple and takes just minutes. For special effects, try crimping decorative vellums, handmade papers, and surface designed papers.

1 Trim your paper to no wider than the width of your crimper's rollers less ¼ inch (6 mm). The length can be as long as you like.

2 Insert one end of the paper between the front and back rollers.

3 Lightly squeeze the crimper's handle and slowly turn the handle in a clockwise direction.

4 For tighter crimps, place your index finger at the top of the handle and firmly squeeze the handle while rolling.

basic techniques

simple weaving

The basic technique of over-under weaving creates distinctive results, but don't stop there. Play with the width of your strips, as well as the weaving pattern.

1 Start by cutting weaving strips from at least two colors of paper. You can cut the strips as wide or as narrow as you like, although ³/8- to ³/4 inch strips (9 to 18 mm) work especially well.

2 Arrange strips from one color side by side, oriented vertically, on your work surface, leaving a little space between each strip. Secure the strips at the top with tape.

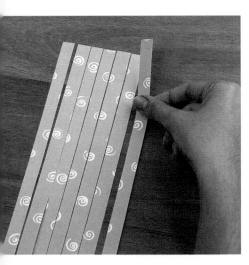

3 Starting at one side, begin weaving in strips of another color(s), working them over and under in a repeatable pattern. (Note: Feel free to vary the pattern by going over two, under two, or over two, under one, etc.).

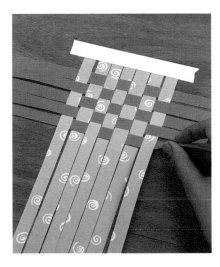

4 When you've woven the entire area, take a minute to "tighten" up the strips, pulling them together to eliminate gaps between them.

weaving variations

For a different look, try varying the shapes of your paper strips.

1 Working with a large sheet of paper, cut wavy strips into the paper, about ¹/2 to ³/4 inch (12 to 18 mm) wide, stopping just short of the top edge of the paper.

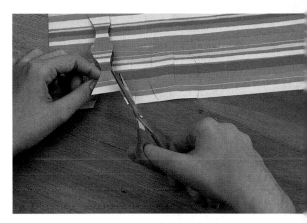

2 Tape the top, uncut length of the paper to your weaving surface, then begin weaving in strips as directed in Step 3, above.

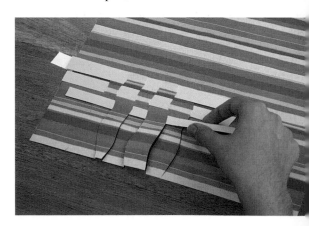

Crimped & Quilled Duck Gift Bag

Good things come in small packages—so why shouldn't the small packages be special, too? Pretty paper bags are perfect for holding party favors for wedding and baby showers. And this sweet little duck is so easy to make, you can use it to adorn guest books, cards, candles and all kinds of other products to create a splashy party theme.

materials

Card stock in orange, yellow, and blue

Clear-drying craft glue

Scrap of black paper

Small white gift bag

Scissors

Personal paper trimmer or scissors

Personal paper crimper

Ruler

Hatpin or toothpick

Decorative paper punch, ⅛-inch (3 mm) circle

Designer: Molly Smith

step by step

1 Each part of the duck—the beak, the head, the body, and the wing—and each wave is made by rolling a single, ¼-inch-wide (6 mm) strip of card stock into a circle, and, for some parts, shaping that circle. Start by cutting the strips as follows:

1 yellow strip for the head, measuring 10 inches (15 cm) long

1 yellow strip for the body, measuring 24 inches (61 cm) long

1 yellow strip for the wing, measuring 12 inches (30.5 cm) long

1 orange strip for the beak, measuring 3 inches (7.5 cm) long

3 blue strips for the waves, each measuring 3 inches (7.5 cm) long

2 Use your personal paper trimmer to trim the strips to ¼ inch (6 mm) wide. Then run each strip through your paper crimper.

3 Next, working on one strip at a time, form the strips into circles with the hatpin or toothpick: Start at one end of a strip and roll the paper tightly around the hatpin. Place the resulting circle on a flat surface and allow the tension to release until the circle reaches the specified diameter:

Head: ¾ inch (2 cm)

Body: 2 inches (5 cm)

Wing: 1¼ inches (3 cm)

Beak: ⅜ inch (9.5 mm)

(NOTE: Because the waves won't be glued into circles, they don't need to be a particular diameter.)

4 To secure the circles that will be part of the duck, apply a dab of glue to the loose end of the strip and press it

(continued on following page)

against the outside of the circle. Don't glue the circles that will be waves, though; as you can see from the photo, their ends should stay loose. Allow the glue to dry.

5 To make the wing, hold the 1¼-inch (3 cm) circle in both hands and pinch one end to form a teardrop shape.

6 To make the duck's body, form the 2-inch (5 cm) circle into a teardrop shape as described above. Then create the tail by pushing down on one side of the teardrop while pulling and curling the end of the tail up.

7 Make the beak by pinching one side of the ⅜-inch (9.5 mm) circle.

8 Using the photo as a guide, assemble and glue the duck pieces together (but not to the bag yet), placing the wing on top of the body.

9 Make the duck's eye by punching a ⅛-inch (3 mm) circle from the scrap of black paper. Glue it in place.

10 Allow the duck to dry for a few minutes; then glue it and the waves to the bag. Let the glue dry completely before filling the bag with goodies.

Quilled Hearts

These pretty paper hearts will add a little old-fashioned romance wherever you see fit to use them—on scrapbooks, cards, or just scattered artfully about your home. For an unusual effect, choose a snazzy specialty paper with glitter or embroidery and crimp it before quilling.

Designer: Molly Smith

materials

Decorative paper in the colors and textures of your choice

Clear-drying craft glue

Personal paper trimmer or scissors

Paper crimper, (optional)

Scissors

Ruler

Hatpin or toothpick

step by step

1 For each heart, cut a strip of paper about 6 inches (15 cm) long and trim it to ⅜ inch (9.5 mm) wide. You can make larger hearts by using longer strips of paper or by gluing two strips of paper together, over lapping their ends a bit.

2 Run the paper strip through your paper crimper, if desired.

3 Fold the paper strip in half.

4 Use the hatpin or toothpick to shape the heart: Start at one end of the strip and roll the paper tightly around the hatpin to about 1½ inch (3.8 cm) from the fold. Remove the pin and repeat at the other end of the strip. (To create scroll shapes rather than hearts, just roll the second end in the opposite direction.)

5 Place the heart on a flat surface and allow the tension in the curled ends to release evenly.

6 Use your hands to shape the heart as desired. When you're happy with its shape, apply a small dab of glue between the two curled ends and press them together to secure. Allow the glue to dry before gluing the heart to another project.

Crimped and quilled shapes make fun, easy mobiles: just string them together with a needle and thread, securing in place with clear-drying craft glue.

Paper Bead Jewelry

Fashion your own beads and jewelry from your favorite decorative papers. The beads can be fun and funky or reserved and elegant — just choose a paper style that suits your fancy.

Paper, preferably colorful and
without texture

Scissors

Rounded toothpick, wire coat
hanger, or small skewer

Clear-drying craft glue

Gold/Silver leaf paint (optional)

Craft wire

Polyurethane spray

Elastic jewelry cord

Sewing needle

Plastic or glass beads (optional)

1 Begin by cutting your paper. (See patterns.) Cutting a long triangle will make a tapered bead. For a slightly different look, cut the tips off the triangles. For a cylinder shape, cut your paper into a long rectangle. Vary the sizes of widths and lengths to create smaller or larger beads.

2 Roll your paper—large end first—around the toothpick, wire coat hanger, or skewer as tightly as possible. As you roll, occasionally dot the back side of the paper with glue to hold the bead in place. Use a small amount of glue again at the tip. Allow the glue to completely dry.

3 For added sparkle, paint accents of gold or silver leaf paint onto your beads. Allow the paint to dry.

4 String the beads onto a length of craft wire. Secure the wire from a clothesline or tree limb to ensure even coverage, then spray with several coats of polyurethane, allowing each coat to completely dry before adding the next.

5 Thread the elastic jewelry string through a sewing needle, knot the other end, and string your paper beads. Alternate beads of different sizes, shapes, and colors, adding plastic or glass beads if desired.

6 Knot the other end of the string and tie the ends together.

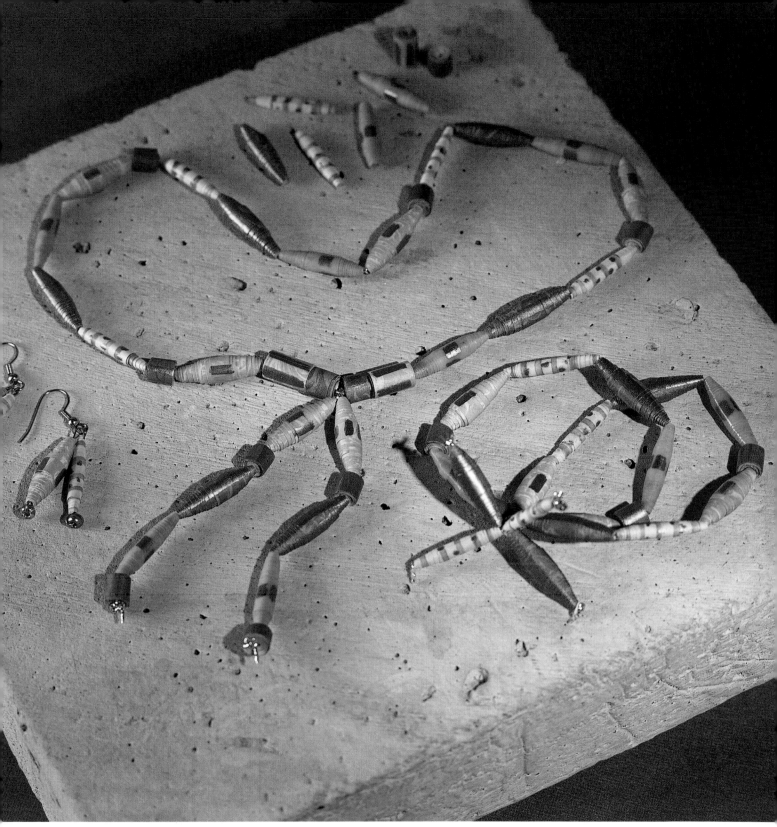

Designer: Susan Greenelsh

Woven Paper Placemats

It only seems as if pre-made placemats come in endless patterns and colors. As soon as you try to find one that's just right for your kitchen, you'll discover that your choices are sadly limited. Fortunately, where there's paper, there's a way. In about the same amount of time you'd spend shopping for the perfect placement, you can make your own.

materials

(Enough for two placemats)

2 sheets of dark blue vellum paper, each measuring 12 x 12 inches (30.5 x 30.5 cm)

2 sheets of medium blue vellum paper, each measuring 12 x 12 inches

1 sheet of pale blue vellum paper, measuring 12 x 12 inches

1 sheet of pale green vellum paper, 12 x 12 inches

1 sheet of yellow vellum paper, 12 x 12 inches

Paper cutter or a craft knife, straight edge, and cutting mat

Scissors

Paper clips

Laminate pouch, measuring 11 x 17 inches (28 x 43 cm) (available at copy shops)

Heat laminator (available for use at copy shops)

step by step

1 Start by cutting six strips measuring ½ inch (1.3 cm) wide and 12 inches long from each sheet of paper. Then cut six more ½-inch-wide strips from each sheet of paper, these measuring 9 inches long.

2 Arrange 16 of the 12-inch strips side by side, oriented horizontally on your work surface, leaving about ½ inch between each strip. Arranged this way, the strips will form a rectangle measuring about 15 inches tall and, of course, 12 inches long. (You can alternate the colors however you'd like, or follow the pattern shown in the project photo.)

3 Starting at one end of the rectangle formed by the 12-inch strips, weave one of the 9-inch strips vertically over and under the 12-inch strips. You may want to use a paper clip at each end of the shorter strip to hold the pieces in place as you continue to work.

4 Repeat Step 3 with a second 9-inch strip. Continue adding 9-inch strips this way until you've woven the entire rectangle; this will probably take about 21 9-inch strips.

5 When you've woven the entire rectangle, take a minute to "tighten" up the strips, pulling them together to eliminate gaps between them. (If you used paper clips earlier, remove them before tightening the pieces.)

6 Repeat Steps 2–5 to make a second placemat. You should have about 10 12-inch

Designer: Diana Light

strips left. You can save these for another project, or cut them into ½-inch squares to use as decorative accents along the sides of the woven rectangles.

7 Carefully slip each woven rectangle into a laminate

pouch. If you're using the ½-inch squares from Step 6, arrange them inside the pouches, too, along the placemats' vertical edges.

8 Laminate the pouches with the heat laminator

at your local copy shop, following the manufacturer's instructions. When the placemats have cooled, trim the excess plastic with a craft knife or scissors to achieve the desired finished size.

Beaded Curtain

So, you've made some incredible scrapbooks, journal covers, and paper lamp-shades. Once the projects are finished, though, what should you do with all those marvelous bits of scrap paper? Beaded curtains, of course! The same techniques can also be used to create Christmas tree garlands.

materials

Assorted printed papers in colors of your choice

Paper cutter or metal ruler and craft knife

Small dowel, approximately ⅜-inch (1 cm) in diameter*

Fine-tip artist's paintbrush

Decoupage medium, any finish

Clear monofilament

Scissors

Colored faceted beads or beads of your choice, 10 mm

Hot glue and hot glue gun

Clear faceted beads or beads of your choice, 12 mm

Assorted scallop edge spacer beads or spacer beads of your choice

Clear oval tube beads, ¾ inch (2 cm)

step by step

1 Use the paper cutter or metal ruler and craft knife to cut uniform strips of the printed papers. The paper beads in the pictured project were made from 1¼ x 8½-inch (2.8 x 21.6 cm) strips, although you can adjust the width of the strips if you would like shorter beads. You may cut all the strips needed for your project now (approximately 11 paper beads for each length in a curtain that is 24 inches [61 cm] long), or cut additional strips as required.

2 Evenly roll the end of one paper strip around the ⅜-inch (1 cm) dowel. As soon you make one full rotation, use the artist's paintbrush to apply decoupage medium across the paper where it connects. Hold the wrapped paper together a few seconds until the adhesive begins to bond, wiping off any excess glue if necessary.

3 Tightly and evenly continue to roll the paper around the dowel until you reach the end. Apply a thin line of decoupage medium across the end off the paper, press it down to secure, and hold together until bonded. Gently slide the paper bead off the dowel. Set the bead aside and let dry.

4 Repeat Steps 2 and 3 to create beads out of all the paper strips you've cut. You may want to separate beads from different papers into groups. This will help you stay organized when stringing the beads later.

5 Cut a piece monofilament that is approximately 6 inches (15 cm) longer than the length of the curtain. The excess line will be used to make a loop so the strand of beads can hang from the curtain rod. (It's always better to err on the side of cutting too much line rather than not cutting enough; you can always trim off any excess.) Tie a knot in the end of the line.

6 String one 10-mm colored faceted bead or bead of your choice onto the monofilament and guide it down to the knot. Once the bead is in position, secure it to the knot with a dab of hot glue, and let dry.

7 Add one 12-mm clear faceted bead, a scallop edge spacer bead, and a second clear faceted bead to the strand. Select the paper bead of your choice, and string it on the line. Follow this with one 12-mm clear faceted bead, a scallop edge spacer bead, and another clear faceted bead. Repeat this sequence until you have beaded a strand of the desired length, finishing with a 12-mm clear faceted bead.

8 Add a 10-mm colored faceted bead or bead of your choice to the end of the strand. Gently push the beads together, taking any slack out of the line. Use a dab of hot glue to secure the last colored bead in position on the monofilament, and let dry.

9 String one ¾-inch clear oval tube bead on the monofilament line. Take the end of the line and thread it back through the top hole of the bead, leaving a loop of line large enough to go over the curtain rod. Tie a knot in the line directly under the tube bead, and clip off any excess monofilament.

10 Repeat Steps 5 through 9 to make as many length of beaded curtain you need to cross your window or doorway. As you make each strand, you may want to vary the order of the bead's paper patterns as well as the order of the color of the spacer beads. Hang the strands on the curtain rod and enjoy!

Designer: Marthe Le Van

Woven Heart Envelopes

These easy-to-weave hearts are a great way to use up scraps of your favorite decorative papers, and the finished hearts can be used to hold Valentine treats, envelopes for scrapbooking pages, or card decorations.

materials

1 sheet each of two
   different decorative papers

Ruler and pencil

Scissors

step by step

1 Cut a 3- x 8-inch (7.5 x 20 cm) rectangle from each of your decorative papers, then fold each paper in half so they're 3 x 4 inches (7.5 x 10 cm).

2 Trace one of the templates from page 303 onto each piece of paper, positioning the half-circle end of the template on the unfolded edge of the paper. Cut out the shapes.

3 Starting at the folded edge, measure and cut two slits in each piece of folded paper 1 inch (2.5 cm) apart and 3¼ inches (8 cm) long (figure 1).

4 Weave the strips from each paper together in an over-under pattern, referring to figures 2 and 3. Adjust the curve of each half of the heart by tightening or loosening the weaving until you're happy with the heart shape and have a snug fit.

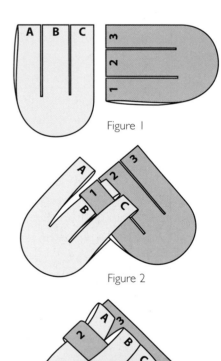

Figure 1

Figure 2

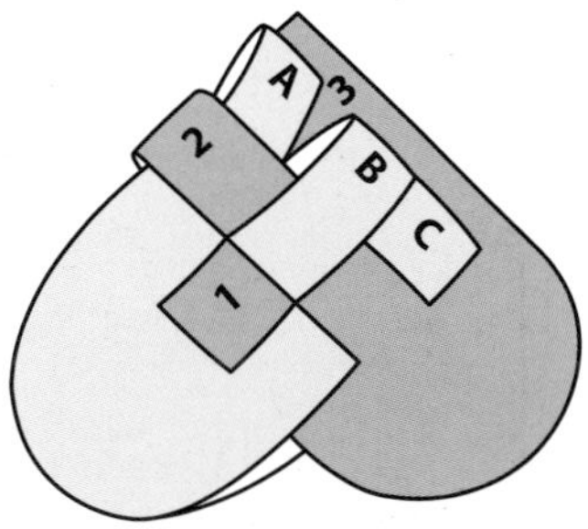

Figure 3

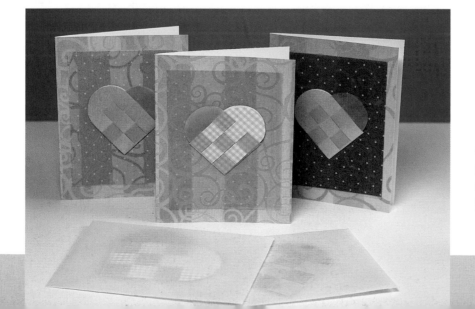

Woven hearts were glued to the front of a handcrafted card. The envelope is a great place to tuck a personal note or treat.

Designer: Shannon Yokeley

Designer: Susan Greenelsh

Woven Paper Napkin Rings

Remember weaving long lengths of gum wrappers as a teenager? The process was relaxing and fun, but you never ended up with something use could actually use. These napkin ring holders use the same simple folding and weaving techniques, but are both practical and pretty.

materials

Ruler and pencil

Scissors or paper cutter

Several colors of light- to medium-weight paper

Sheet of vellum

Bone folder

Clear-drying craft glue

Paper clips

step by step

1 Carefully measure and cut your paper into 4½- x ½-inch (11.5 x 1.25 cm) strips. You will need 13 to 19 strips per napkin ring

2 Fold each strip in half at the center. Open the fold, then press each side of the strip toward the center. Use the bone folder to make each fold crisp.

3 Hold a folded strip (Strip A) with the open end down and hold another folded strip (Strip B) with the open end facing toward the first strip at a 90-degree angle.

4 Slip the folded ends between the inside and outside of the fold on each edge. Slide Strip B snugly against the top center fold of the Strip A.

5 Slip another strip between the inside and outside of the edges up through Strip B. Continue building the strips together in this manner, back and forth in a zigzag pattern, until you're happy with the length. End with an odd number of strips.

6 Place a small amount of non-toxic glue between the folds of the last strip. Form a circle with the woven papers by placing the first strip between the open folds of the last one, and carefully secure it together using the paper clips. Allow the glue to completely.

tip *While you're in the paper-folding mood, make several 6-inch (15 cm) lengths for curtain tie-backs.*

Curlicue Paper Lamp Shade

Let's face it: The average lampshade just doesn't have a lot of personality. With this easy project, though, you can turn the usual boring bulb topper into a decorative centerpiece.

materials

Lampshade in need of pizzazz

Heavy-weight art paper in two tones of the same colors

Paper clips

Clear-drying craft glue

Silver brads

Cloth measuring tape

Scissors

Paintbrush

Craft knife

step by step

1 Start by measuring the lampshade's circumference at its upper (narrower) end. Use a pencil to make light tick marks on the shade, dividing it into an even number of ¾-inch (1.9 cm) intervals. You'll use these marks as guide for placing the paper strips.

2 Decide which color of paper you'd like to use to make the curlicue strips. (In the project shown, the lighter color is used for the curlicues and the darker color is used for the "background" stripes.) Cut this paper into strips about ¾ inch wide and about 7 inches (18 cm) longer than the lampshade is tall. (For example, if your shade is 7 inches tall, your strips should be 14 inches [35.5 cm] long.)

3 Cut an equal number of ¾-inch-wide strips from the other color of paper, making these strips 2 inches (5 cm) longer than your lampshade is tall.

4 To curl the curlicue strips, simply wind about 6 inches (15 cm) of the bottom of a strip tightly around the shaft of a pencil. Unroll the strip and repeat until you've curled all the strips of this color.

5 Begin attaching the curlicue strips to the shade. Fold over the top inch (2.5 cm) of the flat end of one of the curled strips. Then, on the inside surface of the top end of the lampshade, paint a thin coat of glue over the section where you'll attach the strip.

6 Slip the folded end of the curled strip over the top edge of the lampshade, pressing the folded flap firmly against the glue on the inside of the lampshade. Secure the strip with a paper clip while the glue dries.

7 Repeat Steps 4 and 5, attaching a curled strip at every other ¾-inch interval until you've completed a full circle around the shade.

8 Next, attach the remaining strips. Fold about an inch over at one end of a strip. Apply glue to the top inside of the lampshade and attach the strip just as you attached the curlicue strips. Secure the top

end of the strip with a paper clip, then apply glue to the bottom inside of the lampshade where the strip's other end will attach. Fold the bottom end of the strip over the edge of the lampshade, and press it in place against the glued surface. Secure this end with a paper clip, too.

9 Repeat Step 7 to attach the remaining strips. Allow the glue to dry thoroughly, then remove the paper clips.

10 To attach the silver brads, use a craft knife to cut a small slit centered at the top of each strip. Insert a brad in each slit through the front side of the lampshade. Then fold the brad's wings back to fasten.

11 Slip your newly glorious lampshade over a worthy lamp, flip the switch, and behold the glory.

Designer: Kathryn Temple

263

Designer: Molly Smith

Crimped Paper Monogram

Adapt the centuries'-old needlework tradition of monogramming to your favorite paper craft. You can shape your monogram letter freehand, or use a printed letter as a pattern. Frame your finished monogram or use it on a scrapbooking page or gift card.

materials

Wood frame with a 4- to 5-inch (10 to 12.5 cm) opening

Sand paper

Pink acrylic paint

Sponge brush

White card stock or construction paper

Clear-drying craft glue

Personal paper trimmer

Paper crimper

Silver leafing pen

Background paper

Scissors

Ruler

Hat pin or toothpick

Wax paper and printed letter (optional)

step by step

1 Sand and paint the frame using the sponge brush. Allow to completely dry, then add a second coat.

2 Trim two pieces of white construction paper to $\frac{1}{2}$- x 11-inch 1.25 x 28 cm) strips. Glue the strips together at one end, overlapping slightly, to form a 22-inch (56 cm) strip. After the glue has completely dried, run the 22-inch strip through the paper crimper.

3 Create your chosen letter by shaping the crimped paper strip, cutting the strip into shorter lengths and piecing them together as necessary. To make a spiral, roll up to 4 inches of the end of the paper tightly around the hat pin or toothpick, then lay flat and allow the tension to release. You can unroll and loosely re-roll the paper with your fingers until you're happy with the size of the spiral.

4 If you prefer to work with a pattern, enlarge your chosen letter on a photocopier and place it under a sheet of wax paper. Shape your crimped strip over the letter, gluing as needed. After the glue has completely dried, use the tip of the hat pin to release the letter from the wax paper.

5 Insert the background paper into frame opening. Glue the quilled letter onto the background paper, then highlight the top edge of the letter with the silver leafing pen.

Woven Boxes

These decorative boxes are as versatile as they are beautiful. Make them from wedding papers to hold guest favors, or from holiday papers as gift boxes or tree ornaments. Create larger or smaller boxes by adjusting the size of the template.

materials

Two colors of contrasting construction paper or heavy scrapbooking paper

Scissors

Craft knife

Clear-drying craft glue

Paper clips

step by step

1 Enlarge and photocopy the box template on page 315. Cut out the template with scissors, then trace the template's shape onto your paper.

2 Fold each of the "arms" of the box shape toward the center to make a crease where the side meets the square that will become the bottom of the box. Fold each arm again 3 inches (7.5 cm) out from the first crease.

3 Use the craft knife to make two vertical cuts, starting at one crease and ending at the other, on each of the four "arms" of the box shape. These cuts can be straight, zig-zagged, or curvy.

4 Cut three 1- x 14-inch (2.5 x 35.5 cm) strips from a different paper color.

5 Use a ruler to mark each of the strips at their 1-, 4-, 7-, 10-, and 13-inch (2.5, 10, 18, 25, and 33 cm) marks. Crease the paper along each of the marks, turning each strip into a square shape.

6 With the sides of your box folded up in the beginnings of a box shape, weave the first strip through the slits you made in the sides, securing the strip in place with a spot of glue. Use a paper clip to hold the strip in place while it dries.

7 Starting from the same corner of the box, weave your second strip through the slits. If you started weaving over the first time around, begin weaving under this time. Repeat with the third strip.

8 Finally, fold the top flaps down, inside the box, and glue them in place, holding them in place with paper clips until dry.

Designer: Kathryn Temple

Christmas Tree Gift Tags

These crimped paper Christmas trees are simple to create. Use them as gift tags, baby's first ornament gifts, or place markers for holiday dinners.

Designer: Molly Smith

materials

Green cardstock or
  construction paper

Clear-drying craft glue

Paper crimper

2-inch (5 cm) tree punch
  or die cut

Gift tag template or die cut

2 eyelets

Eyelet setting tools

Narrow ribbon

Black fine point marker

Scissors

Ruler

Hat pin

Toothpick

step by step

1 Cut seven lengths of ¼-inch-wide (6 mm) paper into 4-inch-long (10 cm) strips.

2 Run each strip through the paper crimper.

3 Roll a length of paper around the hat pin, beginning at one end of the strip and rolling tightly to the end. Lay the pin on a flat surface and allow the tension of circles to release to ⅜ inch (9 mm) in diameter. Repeat with the remaining crimped strips.

4 Glue the end of the strips at their sides to form loose circles. Set aside to dry.

5 Punch out tree and make matching tag using gift tag template.

6 Write a message on each piece if desired and insert eyelet on top of the tree and tag.

7 To make square tree trunk, hold a loose quilled circle in both hands and pinch the sides to form an eye shape. Rotate halfway, then pinch the sides again and shape into a square.

8 Assemble and glue pieces to back of the tree, referring to the photo as a guide.

9 Add ribbon, adjusting the length as needed for a gift tag or tree ornament.

tip *For a more formal look, make the trees from patterned scrapbooking paper, vellum paper, embroidered paper, or metallic paper.*

Use the same technique to make quilled tree ornaments.

Crimped Sunflowers

These crimped and quilled sunflowers make delightful party favors. Position them in miniature clay garden pots filled with candy— but don't overlook their creative potential. Make extras to decorate scrapbooking pages, handmade cards, and journals.

materials

Miniature terra cotta pots

Card stock or construction paper in orange, yellow, red, and brown

Clear-drying craft glue

Personal paper trimmer

Paper crimper

¾-inch (18 mm) circle punch

Scissors

Ruler

Hat pin

Toothpick

Decorative ribbon (optional)

Medium-gauge floral wire and tape (optional)

Silk foliage (optional)

step by step

1 Cut the card stock into ¼-inch (6 mm) strips, then cut the strips to the following lengths: 14 strips of red, yellow, or orange paper cut to 4 inches (10 cm) long for each flower and eight strips of brown paper cut to 8½ inches (23 cm) long for the bloom centers.

2 Run each length of paper through the crimper.

3 Punch out three ¾-inch circles from brown cardstock.

4 Roll each length of paper around the hat pin, beginning at one end of the strip and rolling tightly to the end. Lay the pin on a flat surface to allow the tension of circles to release to ¾ inch for the brown paper and ½ inch for the red, yellow, and orange papers.

5 Apply glue to the ends of the strips at their sides with a toothpick to form loose circles. Allow the glue to dry for 5 minutes.

6 Shape the petals by holding a paper circle in both hands and pinching both sides to make an eye shape.

7 Glue the brown quilled paper to the center of the punched circle. Assemble and glue one end of the petals to center, referring to the photo as a guide.

8 To add a stem, position several silk leaves at the top of a 4-inch (10 cm) length of wire. Secure the leaves against the wire by wrapping with floral wire.

tip

Use piece of waxpaper or acetate for work service. Use toothpick to apply sparingly amounts of glue on all pieces. Slightly moisten end of paper strip before rolling paper around hat pin.

Designer: Molly Smith

Paper Quilling, Rolling & Weaving Gallery

Right: A bouquet of quilled flowers outlines a simple photo frame.
Designer: Malinda Johnston

Below: Remember weaving gum wrappers as a teenager? Use the same simple technique with elegant origami or other patterned papers to make great bracelets.
Designer: Terry Taylor

Above: Create fabulous placemats with a simple over/under weaving technique. To guarantee great results, choose interesting papers and play with placement to form interesting patterns.
Designer: Terry Taylor

Right: Flared paper strips enhance the oval curve of this frame's photo window.
Designer: Malinda Johnston

Below: Small open rolled paper circles frame a larger quilled paper design to form fun, colorful earrings.
Designer: Malinda Johnston

Surface Design

Despite the incredible selection of fabulous papers available today, no self-respecting crafter can resist the urge every now and then to create their own novelty papers. Stamping, embossing, and embroidery are popular ways to embellish paper, and you'll find some great projects for those techniques in this chapter. You'll also find ways to create special effects with miniature glass beads, faux tie-dye, paste paper, and more.

materials

stamps
Stamps are available in so many patterns, sizes, and shapes that you'll soon have a good-sized collection. Be sure to clean your stamps after every use to increase their lifespan.

stamp inks
As the popularity of stamping has increased, so has the selection of colors, pad sizes, and types of ink.

embossing inks
These inks are made with the embossing crafter in mind. They dry much slower than traditional stamping inks.

embossing powder
Embossing powder is made from tiny plastic pellets that melt when heated, allowing them to merge with the stamped ink and create a raised surface. Look for clear, glitter, translucent, and other special-effect powders.

heat gun
This inexpensive tool blows stream of hot air that can be directed at the surfaces you want to emboss.

embroidery needles
As with embroidering on fabric, be sure to choose the smallest possible embroidery needle that works well with the thickness of your paper and the your floss or ribbon to prevent making larger-than-necessary holes in the paper.

embroidery floss & silk ribbon
The best part of shopping for embroidery floss or silk ribbon will be savoring all of the available colors. You can embroidery paper with three strands of cotton embroidery floss or use all six, depending on how delicate you want the finished embroidery to be. Silk ribbons add a lovely touch for more formal paper embroidery projects, such as wedding invitations.

clear-drying craft glue
Secure your paper embroidery on the back side by placing a small amount of glue over knots and loose threads.

paper piercing tool
A tool specifically designed to pierce paper is fine, although the sharp end of your embroidery needle will work just as well. The holes are placed in the paper before you start embroidering to prevent tearing.

basic techniques

stamping
Stamping can transform just about any type of paper from plain to ordinary. The basic techniques are simple to master.

1 Secure the paper you'll be stamping in place with masking tape.

2 Just lightly tap the stamp on the surface of the ink pad; don't press the stamp into the pad or rub it across the pad's top.

3 Test the inked stamp on scrap paper. If the image is too faint, re-ink the stamp; if the stamp is over-inked, blot it on a paper towel.

basic techniques

4 Holding the stamp firmly, press down on the paper without rocking or moving the stamp. Press each corner of the stamp carefully.

5 Lift the stamp straight up without rocking or moving it. Clean the stamp as directed by the manufacturer between colors or after each stamping session.

embossing

Once the trademark of a specialty printing process, embossing still retains its cache, yet is easy for the home crafter to master.

1 To emboss an image, begin by following Steps 1 through 5 above.

2 Immediately after stamping, while the ink is still wet, cover the stamped image with a layer of embossing powder.

3 Shake the excess powder off the stamped image and onto a piece of scrap paper so you can return it to its original container for later use.

4 Turn on your embossing gun and hold it over the embossed surface to activate (melt!) the embossing powder, referring to the manufacturer's instructions. Allow the embossed areas to harden before handling.

Cleaning Stamps

To clean a stamp, simply press it onto a paper towel moistened with water and commercial stamp cleaner. Non-alcohol baby wipes can be used instead, and the moisturizers in them will help condition the rubber.

Some inks will stain your stamps. Don't worry—these stains will not affect the color of future stampings as long as you clean your stamps well between use.

basic techniques

embroidery: chain stitch

The simple chain stitch is a fun variation of the normal up-and-down running stitch virtually everyone knows. The distinctive look of this stitch is created by coming back through the front of the first stitch from underneath as you make the second stitch.

1 Lightly mark the line you'd like to stitch on your paper with a pencil.

2 Use your piercing tool to make holes along your pencil line as shown in the photo below about the length you would like your finished stitches to be. Now add additional holes about a third of the distance of your stitch behind your first stitch holes. If you're a newcomer to embroidery and this makes no sense, don't stop now — just study the photo for a

minute, then practice Steps 3 and 4 on a scrap piece of paper.

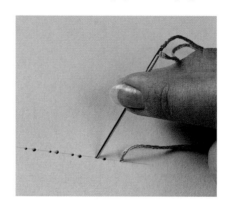

3 Thread your needle and knot the thread. Insert your needle from the back side in the first hole. Pass your needle over the next hole and bring it down the hole after that one. Now, bring your needle up through the hole you just skipped over to create the "chain" effect.

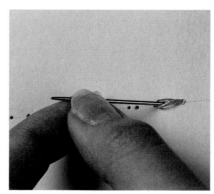

4 Continue the stitch process described in Step 3 until your line of embroidery is as long as you like. Trim the floss on the

back side and secure in place with clear-drying glue.

embroidery: french knots

This classic stitch adds a three-dimensional touch to embroidery projects, and can be mastered in 60 seconds. For a larger or smaller French knot, increase or decrease the number of times you wrap the floss around the needle in Step 2.

1 Make two holes in your paper next to each other with a paper piercing tool or embroidery needle.

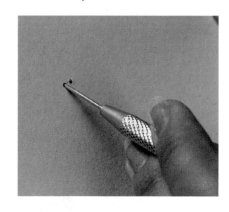

basic techniques

2 Thread and knot the needle with three strands of embroidery floss. Insert the needle into one of the holes from the back side of the paper until the knot rests snugly against the paper. Position the needle about an inch (2.5 cm) up from the bottom of the thread, then spiral the yarn around the needle three times, working from the bottom of the needle up.

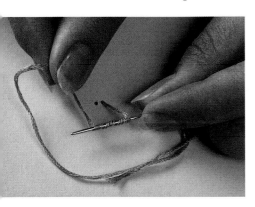

3 Bring the needle back through the paper in the second hole, pulling the needle gently but firmly from the back side, leaving a French knot between the holes.

embroidery: daisy stitch

Embroidered flower petals are easy to create, and look great with a French knot in the center.

1 Make two holes in the paper close together and a third hole about ⅛ to ¼ inch (3 to 6 mm) across from them with your paper piercing tool.

2 Thread and knot the needle, then bring it up from the back side of the paper in one of the two holes that are next to each other. Bring the needle back down through the adjacent hole, leaving about an inch of looped thread on top of the paper (i.e., do not pull the thread all the way through).

3 Bring the needle back to the front side of the paper in the third hole, then insert the needle into the loop (which will become the flower petal) and gently lead it over to the third hole.

4 Gently pull on the thread until the loop rests against the paper, then bring your needle around the loop and back down through the third hole. Trim the floss on the back side and secure in place with clear-drying glue.

279

Paper Sachets

These are definitely not your grandmother's sachets. Undecorated papers are an elegant choice, though it is simple to add rubber-stamped designs or rows of ribbon to create sachets that are your own unique creations.

materials

Unryu papers

Rubber stamp(s)

Stamping ink

Dried herbs or potpourri mix

Decorative-edged scissors

Straight pins

Needle and thread (optional)

Sewing machine (optional)

Double-sided adhesive tape
    (optional)

step by step

1 If desired, rubber stamp designs onto the chosen papers. Here, the designer used a pale lavender color ink to complement the dried lavender tucked inside each sachet. Small, lime green dots were created with a pencil eraser.

2 Cut out two each of simple geometric shapes (squares, rectangles, or even triangles) with decorative-edged scissors. A 4-inch (10 cm) shape is a good beginning size.

3 Pin the two shapes together. By hand or with a sewing machine, stitch all but one side of the shapes together. (If you'd prefer, use double-sided adhesive tape to connect the edges.)

4 Fill the sachets with 2 or 3 tablespoons of dried herbs or potpourri.

5 Sew, tape, or glue the remaining side of the sachet closed.

Designer: Terry Taylor

Designer: Rhonda Black

Tissue-Dyed Butterfly Card

Using plain tissue paper, a little water, and your imagination, you can create an infinite combination of beautiful colors, as individual and special as your gift card's recipient. Use this simple technique to create one-of-a-kind cards to say 'Happy Birthday,' 'Thank You,' or even just 'Happy Spring!'

materials

Coated white card stock

Scissors

4 sheets of card stock, 3 in contrasting solid colors and 1 white

Noncoated tissue paper

Solid butterfly stamp

Watermark ink pad

Lettering or sign stamps and ink pad

Adhesive foam dots

Colored card stock

Glue

Bone folder

Wax paper

Plain folded white card

step by step

1 Use a precut butterfly shaped piece of card stock or cut out your own template from coated white card stock.

2 To tissue-dye the butterfly, tear ragged strips and chunks of noncoated colored tissue paper and position it in intersecting patterns on the coated card stock. Spritz the tissue paper with water. The papers' dye will run and merge in beautiful color combinations, creating a tie-dye effect. Allow to completely dry

3 Remove the tissue strips from the card stock.

4 Use a solid butterfly stamp and watermark-making machine to stamp a watermark butterfly pattern across the card.

5 Using a single sign stamp or several letter stamps, stamp your message on the butterfly.

6 Cut three sheets of colored card stock in progressively smaller sizes. This design shows deep turquoise, bright pink and bright orange layers, each cut $1/16$ inch (1.5 mm) smaller than the previous layer. Glue each layer together, smoothing each with the bone folder to remove wrinkles and air pockets.

7 Glue the card stock layers to the folded white card. Place a sheet of wax paper on the card, and place a heavy book or other heavy flat object on top of the card until the glue completely dries.

8 Mount the butterfly to the layered card stock with the adhesive dots.

Shimmering Glitter Gift Wrap

Jazz up ordinary gift packages in minutes with craft paint, glitter, and a few interesting patterns. If you're having too much fun to stop, make matching gift tags and cards, or replicate the design with frosting on cupcakes.

materials

Unpatterned paper in the colors of your choice

Large, flat work surface

Books or other paperweights

Templates on page 305

Pencil and ruler

Silver and gold puff paints in applicator-tip bottles

Silver glitter

Scrap paper for recycling glitter

step by step

1 Stretch out a length of paper on your work surface, weighting the corners with books or other flat objects, if necessary.

2 Using the templates, lightly trace the larger design elements—the stars and/or spirals—onto the paper with your pencil. Use a ruler to space the pattern evenly over the entire sheet for a more professional look, or work free-form for a more casual result. If a pattern runs off the edge of the paper, allow it to do so.

3 Add starburst shapes, smaller stars, and/or dots in between the larger elements in the design to complete the pattern.

4 Apply the puff paint from the applicator bottles, tracing over the pencil lines. Sprinkle glitter over the paint while it's still wet, working in small sections and allowing each one to dry thoroughly before moving on to the next to prevent smearing the pattern.

5 After the paint has dried, gently shake the excess glitter onto a scrap of paper, then use the paper to funnel the glitter back into its container.

tip *Glitter pens are another easy way to decorate gift wrap paper, as is the old fashioned way of sprinkling glitter over designs made in craft glue.*

Designer: Diana Light

Never-Close-the-Closet Storage Boxes

Although elegant Sunday hats may have gone out of vogue years ago, the fabulous boxes these gorgeous creations came in never go out of storage style and can be found in large craft supply stores for a pittance. Stash your stuff in these decorated boxes and you'll never have to close your closet doors again!

materials

White paper hatbox (available at craft stores)

Watercolor paints in pink and green

Puff paint in pink and green

Gold paint pen

Spray varnish

White craft glue

Gold glitter

Tulle

Fabric tape measure

Pencil

Paintbrush, 1½ inches (3.8 cm) wide (pastry brushes work well, too)

Rolling rubber stamp in a floral pattern, 1½ inches wide or narrower

Pink and gold stamp pads

Large foam fleur de lis stamp

Fine-tipped paintbrush

step by step

1 Start by measuring the circumference of the hatbox and its lid with the fabric measuring tape. Make small tick marks on the box and lid with your pencil at intervals of roughly 1½ inches (3.8 cm). You'll use these tick marks as a guide to paint the pink and green vertical stripes, so make sure to mark off an even number of sections, even if it means the sections are a little larger or smaller than 1½ inches.

2 Using the 1½-inch-wide paintbrush, paint every other section with the pink watercolor paint. Allow the pink paint to dry and clean the brush, then paint the remaining sections with the green watercolor paint. Don't worry if paint overlaps or if there's some white space between the alternating stripes—the puff paint will conceal most of these "mistakes." (See Step 7.)

3 Paint the inside of the hatbox and its lid the same way, alternating stripes of pink and green watercolor. Then paint the top of the lid either solid pink or green.

4 As you can see in the project photo, the pink stripes have a floral pattern. To achieve this effect, ink the rolling rubber stamp on a pink ink pad, and roll a floral stripe over each pink stripe on the outside of both the hatbox and the lid. Allow the ink to dry.

5 Ink the fleur de lis stamp on a gold ink pad, and stamp the design in the center of the box lid's top surface. Let the ink dry.

6 Following the varnish manufacturer's instructions, spray the entire box with varnish and allow it to dry.

Designer: Megan Kirby

7 Using the project photo as a guide, draw lines with the pink or green puff paint between the alternating stripes on the hatbox and lid. Allow the puff paint to dry.

8 Use the gold paint pen to draw stripes on either side of each puff paint line. Let the gold ink dry.

9 Run a line of small, evenly spaced dots of green or pink puff paint along the edge of the lid's top surface. If desired, run another line of puff-paint dots in a second color an inch or two in from the first line. Just be sure to let the first color dry before applying a second color.

10 You can add additional embellishments, such as the tiny flowers at the base of the green stripes and around the top of the pink lid, using the gold paint pen: Draw the flower first, allow the gold ink to dry; then add a dot of puff paint to make the center of the flower.

11 For a final, sparkly touch, use a fine-tipped paintbrush to paint white craft glue over the fleur de lis on the top of the box. Sprinkle gold glitter over the glue. Shake off any excess glitter; then allow the glue to dry.

12 If desired, line the box with tulle before using it.

Paste Paper

Remember how much fun you had finger painting as a child? Making paste papers is a grown-up version of the same technique, except you get to use creative 'tools' in addition to your own fingers. You can work with plain white paper, of course, but colored stock and printed scrapbooking paper also work well and create interesting effects.

materials

Medium-weight paper

Acrylic paint (use concentrated colors for best results)

Paste recipe*

Sponge

Dishpan

Plastic sheeting (optional)

Clothes drying rack or clothesline

Clear plastic drink cups

2-inch-wide (5 cm) brushes

Hair combs, decorative painting tools, sponges—anything that makes interesting texture

step by step

1 Cover a countertop or tabletop with a sheet of heavy plastic.

2 Put several tablespoons of paste into a plastic cup. Slowly add color to the paste with acrylic paint, mixing well, until you're happy with the intensity. Remove any large lumps from the mixture.

3 Fill a dishpan with water. Trim your paper to fit inside the dishpan, then lightly moisten the paper in the water.

4 Lay the paper on your work surface. Use the sponge to remove excess water and to smooth out the paper, then brush the tinted paste onto the damp paper.

5 Use your fingers, combs, forks, or decorative painting tools to draw designs in the paste, exposing the paper underneath. Experiment with 'tools' that you think might add interesting patterns or textures to your paste paper. If you don't like the look, simply re-brush the paste, and start again.

6 Hang the paper to dry with clothespins.

7 When dry, iron the back side of the paper to completely flatten it.

8 Use the finished, one-of-a-kind paper to make your favorite projects in this book!

Designer: Terry Taylor

paste recipe

Enough for about a dozen
   ledger-size sheets of paper

3 cups cool water

4 tablespoons white cake flour

3 tablespoons white rice flour

1 tablespoon glycerin
   (available at pharmacies)

Liquid dish detergent

Blend the two flours in a saucepan.

Add a little water at a time to the flour mixture, stirring well with a fork or wooden spoon until there are no lumps.

Add the remainder of the water, then cook the mixture over medium heat, stirring constantly.

Bring the mixture almost to a boil (small bubbles will appear around the edges).

Reduce the heat and cook an additional three minutes.

Remove the saucepan from the heat. Add the glycerin and a drop or two of dish detergent. Stir well.

Leftover paste can be stored tightly covered in the refrigerator until needed.

Embroidered Paper Garden Card

This multitechnique card features embroidery, paper punching, and paper cutting. You can adapt the colors and patterns to create wedding, Valentine, and Christmas cards.

materials

Card stock

Decorative paper in 3 solid colors and 1 pattern

Bone folder

Embroidery floss

Needle

Awl or paper piercer

Scissors

Ruler and pencil

Floral paper punch

Hole punch

Decorative-edged scissors

Clear-drying craft glue or sticker machine

step by step

1 Cut a 6 ½- x 10-inch (16.5 x 25 cm) piece of piece of card stock and a 1-inch-wide (2.5 cm) strip of card stock. Fold the card in half and smooth the crease with a bone folder.

2 Use decorative-edged scissors to trim the bottom front edge of the card.

3 Punch several floral shapes from two of your solid papers and set them aside.

4 Use the negative shape left over from punching as a template. Place the template on the front of the card, referring to the photo as a guide. Mark the points of each flower petal, then make corresponding marks in the center. Mark as many flowers as desired. Pierce the marks with a needle or awl.

5 Separate your embroidery floss into two three-strand lengths, then make flower petals. (See page 279 for basic stitching instructions.)

6 Punch circles from the solid paper colors, and adhere them to the centers of the embroidered flowers.

7 Cut the strip of card stock into squares and cover the back side of the stitched flowers.

8 Adhere a 1-inch-wide strip of patterned paper to the inside bottom of the card.

9 Adhere your punched flower shapes to the front of the card, referring to the photo as a guide.

10 To create a matching decorative envelope, embellish the envelope with punched flowers and a strip of patterned decorative paper.

Designer: Terry Taylor

Designer: Rhonda Black

Glass Bead Card

Remember how much fun it was to make cards with glitter and glue as a child? Have the same fun with a more elegant effect using tiny glass beads to create this beautiful card. The beads reflect the edges of the image, making the image appear to move and shimmer, creating a memorable card for any occasion.

materials

Three sheets of solid card stock, two in contrasting colors and one white

Stamp and black waterproof ink pad

Markers

Glue

Sheet of double-sided adhesive

Bone folder

Catch tray or open box

Miniature clear and single-colored glass beads

1/8 inch (32 mm) double-sided adhesive tape

Wax paper

step by step

1 Trim the white card stock to 4 x 5¼ inches (10 x 13 cm, then stamp your image in black waterproof ink. Color the image with markers.

2 Cut second piece of card stock about ½ inch (1.25 cm) larger than your stamped card stock. Center and glue the two pieces together, using the bone folder to smooth wrinkles and air pockets. Allow the glue to completely dry.

3 Cut a sheet of double-sided adhesive to the size of your stamped card stock. Place the adhesive over the image and smooth out any wrinkles or air pockets with the bone folder.

4 Peel off the protective film and place the card in a tray to collect stray glass beads.

5 Pour clear miniature beads over the surface and press the beads onto the surface with your fingertips until the entire taped surface is covered.

6 Carefully edge the larger card stock with double-sided tape. Return the card to your catch tray and pour tiny colored beads over the entire tape border, pressing the beads in place.

7 Fold a piece of 11- x 6¾-inch (30 x 17 cm) card stock in half, using the bone folder to crease the paper. Glue the beaded assembly to the front of the folded card stock.

8 Place a piece of wax paper over the card, and stack a heavy book or other flat heavy object over the card until the glue has completely dried.

Surface Design Sampler Blocks

Simple wood blocks provide multiple surfaces to showcase your favorite decorative papers and stamped and embossed patterns. To display, simply stack the blocks in an interesting arrangement on a shelf or desk.

materials

5 2-inch (5 cm) wooden blocks

3 sheets of contrasting decorative paper, one dark, one light, and one textured

2 small paintbrushes

Acrylic gold paint

10 decorative images, 5 small and 5 large (look for images in clip art books or in magazines.)

Scissors

Gold and black stamp ink

Gold and black embossing powder

3 rubber stamps in varying sizes

Embossing gun

Quick-drying craft glue

step by step

1 Cut four 2-inch squares from each of the decorative papers.

2 Paint two opposing sides gold and allow to completely dry.

3 Paint the back side of each type of decorative paper with glue, then center each on one side of the block, positioning the dark and textured papers on opposite sides.

4 Enlarge or reduce your images if necessary. The large image should be roughly the size of a block side, while the small image should be about half that size. Carefully trim out a large and a small image, and glue them on top of the dark and textured decorative papers.

5 Using the smaller rubber stamps and gold ink, stamp images on the light-colored paper, allowing them to overlap. These images will be flat, but leave room on each block to include at least one more stamping that will be embossed.

6 Using the largest rubber stamp and black ink, stamp an image on a gold-painted side of the block. Immediately apply black embossing powder, then use the embossing gun to achieve a raised surface. Allow to completely dry. Repeat on remaining gold-painted side.

7 Stamp one or two more gold images next to and/or overlapping the black embossed images. Immediately

Designer: Suzie Millions

apply gold embossing powder, then use the embossing gun to achieve a raised surface. Allow to completely dry.

 Repeat Steps 1 through 10 with the remaining blocks.

tip *For extra-smooth gluing, place a clean sheet of scrap paper on top of your newly glued paper and gently smooth down. Remove the scrap paper, then wipe off any excess glue with a damp paper towel.*

Embossed Botanicals Cards

The three-dimensional effect created with embossing enhances the fine lines of the floral and herbal stamps used in these cards. The technique is so simple you can make a matching gift tag in less than five minutes.

materials

Neutral-colored card stock

Decorative-edged scissors

Bone folder

Scrap paper

Rubber stamps

Stamp pad

Embossing powder

Heat gun

step by step

1 Cut a card shape from the card stock using the decorative-edged scissors. Fold the card in half and smooth with a bone folder.

2 Stamp an image onto a piece of scrap paper from Step 1. Immediately cover the stamped image with embossing powder, then shake the excess powder from the card onto a piece of scrap paper and return it to its original container.

3 If you're happy with the effect achieved in Step 2, repeat the process on the front of your card, adding powder and removing it from one stamped image before stamping another

4 Use the heat gun to activate (melt) the embossing powder, taking care to cover all of the stamped areas.

NOTE: Remember to cover your stamped image IMMEDIATELY with embossing powder. If you wait until the ink dries, the powder will not adhere.

tip *Increase the visual interest of your embossed projects by embossing some of the images and leaving others simply stamped.*

Designer: Megan Kirby

Surface Design Gallery

Above: Bring a handful of blank cards and some crayons with you on your next vacation, then preserve interesting sights by making rubbings on the card fronts. Designer: Dana Irwin

Below: A favorite pocket watch stamp served as inspiration for this hourglass die-cut accordion book. Designer: Julia Monroe

Above: One-of-a-kind stationery sets are easy to create for gifts (or, better yet, for yourself!) with stamped and embossed images. Designer: Kinga Britschgi

Left: A Japanese-style lattice room divider makes a great surface to showcase stamped and embossed papers. Designer: Katherine Aimone

Below left: Looking for a special gift box (and a good excuse to play with your stamps)? These decorative boxes combine ribbon, stamping, and embellishment with spectacular results. Designer: Judi Kauffman

Below right: Love stamping and feeling adventurous? Carve your own stamps from linoleum with inexpensive carving tools. Designer: Emily Wilson Hintz

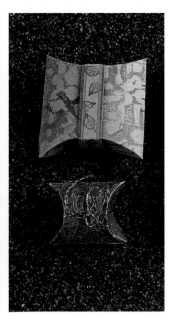

templates

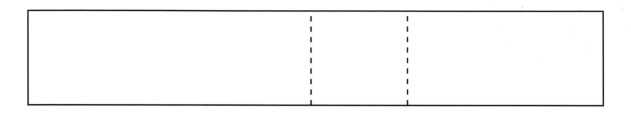

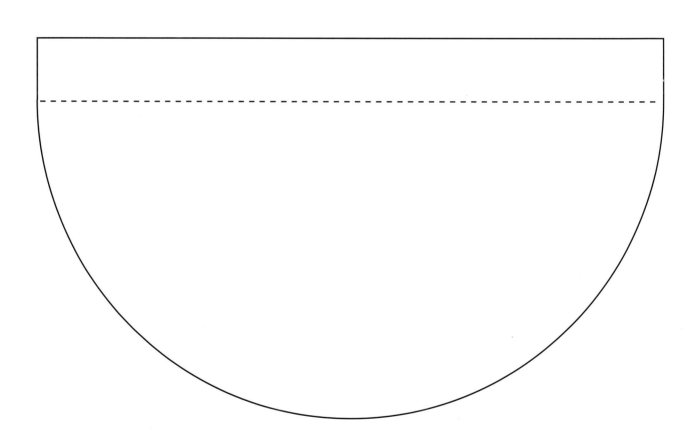

Page 140, Gift Bag
(photocopy at 100%)

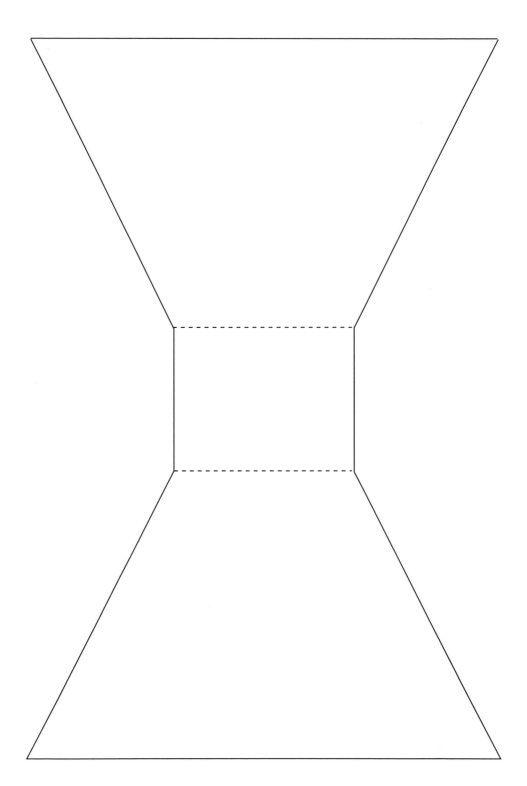

Page 140, Gift Bag
(photocopy at 130%)

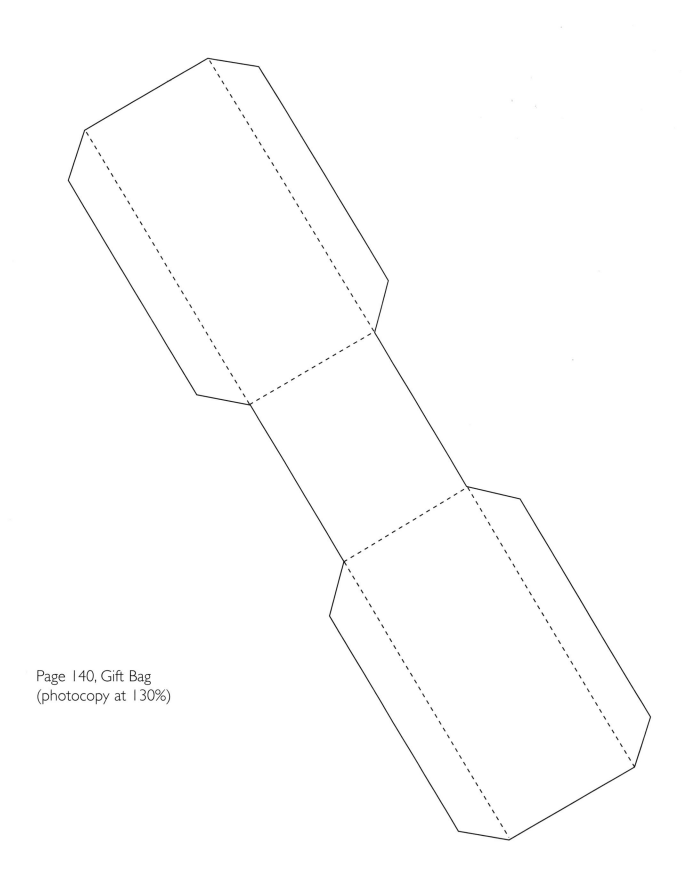

Page 140, Gift Bag
(photocopy at 130%)

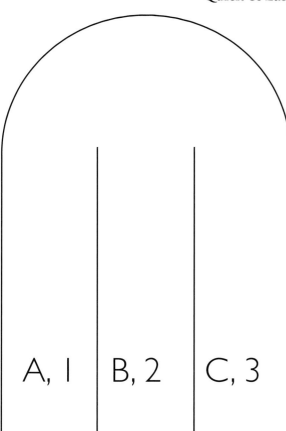

A, 1

B, 2

C, 3

A, 1 | B, 2 | C, 3

A, 1

B, 2

C, 3

Page 258, Woven Heart Envelopes
(photocopy at 100%)

A, 1

B, 2

C, 3

Page 234, Paper Sculpture Angels
(photocopy at 100%)

Page 232, Sparkling Star Ornaments
(photocopy at 100%)

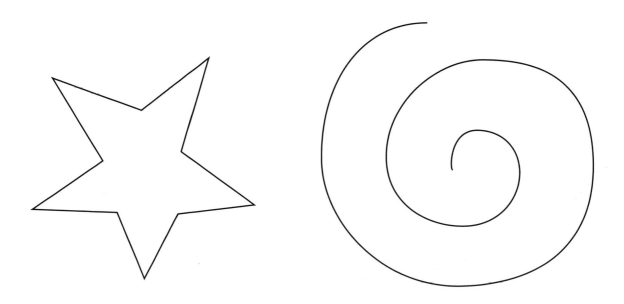

Page 285, Shimmering Gliiter Gift Wrap
(photocopy at 100%)

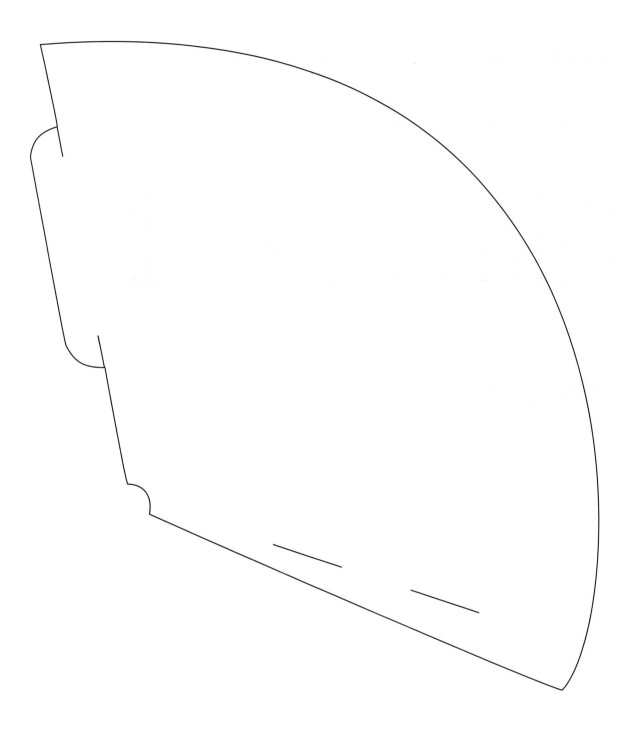

Page 136, Playful Party Hats
(photocopy at 130%)

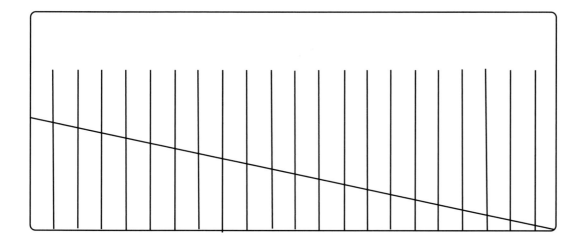

Page 136, Playful Party Hats
(photocopy at 100%)

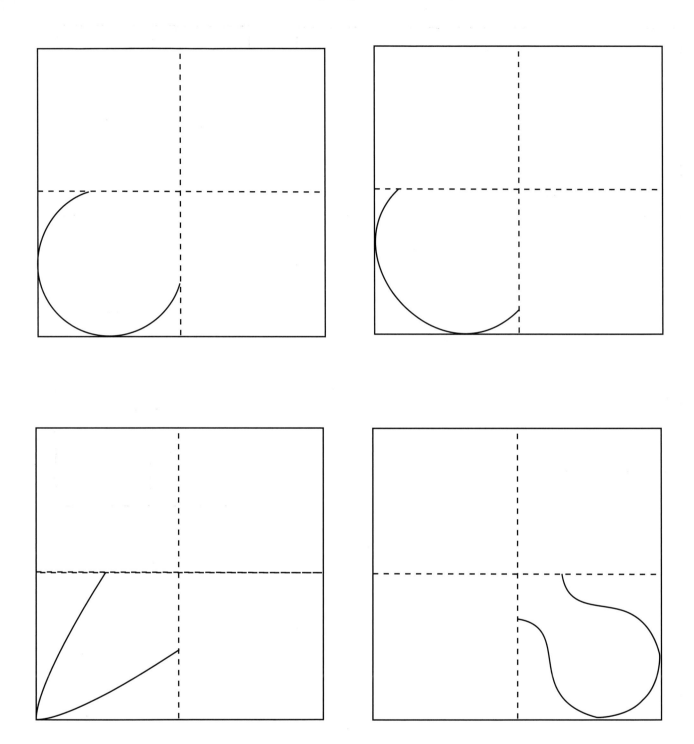

Page 224, Luminous Vellum Flower Garland
(photocopy at 100%)

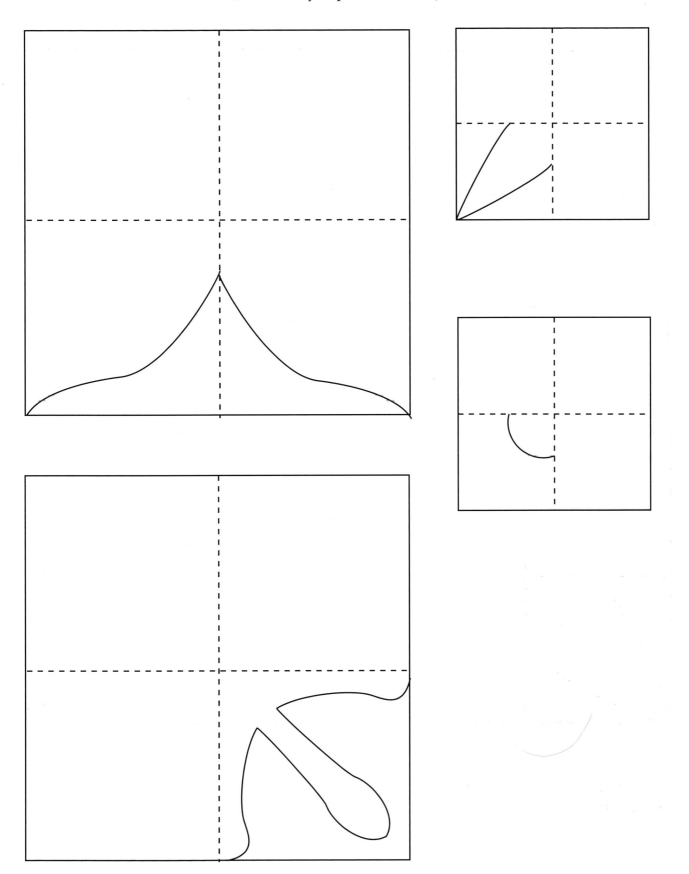

Page 236, Marvelous Mock Stained Glass
(photocopy at 200%)

Page 236, Marvelous Mock Stained Glass
(photocopy at 200%)

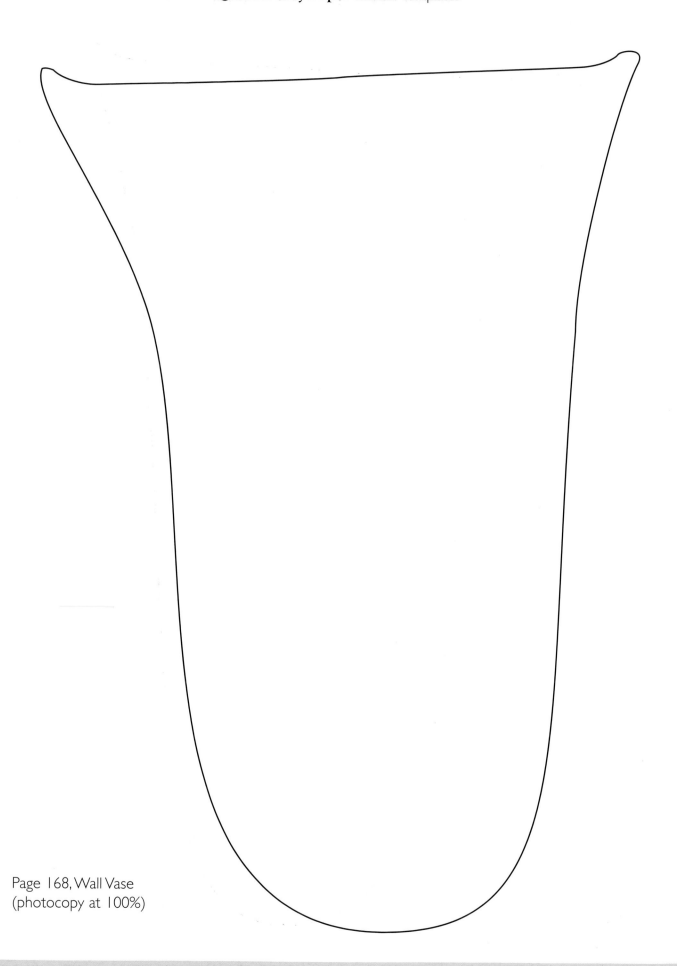

Page 168, Wall Vase
(photocopy at 100%)

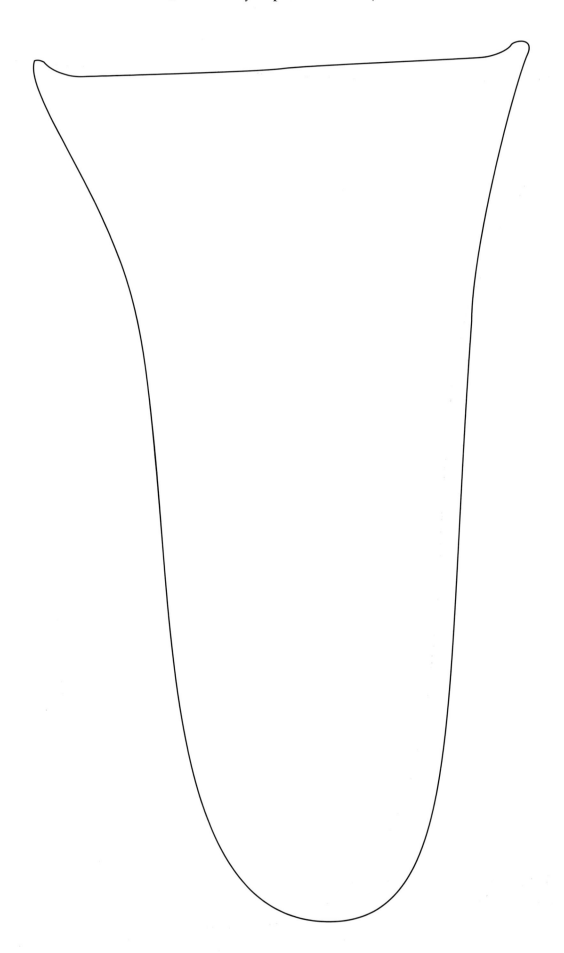

Page 158, Paper Clay Dragonflies
(photocopy at 100%)

Page 266, Woven Boxes
(photocopy at 200%)

A	B	C	D	E	F	G	H	A	B	A	H	G	F	E	D	C	B	A
B	C	D	E	F	G	H	A	B	C	B	A	H	G	F	E	D	C	B
C	D	E	F	G	H	A	B	C	D	C	B	A	H	G	F	E	D	C
D	E	F	G	H	A	B	C	D	E	D	C	B	A	H	G	F	E	D
E	F	G	H	A	B	C	D	E	F	E	D	C	B	A	H	G	F	E
F	G	H	A	B	C	D	E	F	G	F	E	D	C	B	A	H	G	F
G	H	A	B	C	D	E	F	G	H	G	F	E	D	C	B	A	H	G
H	A	B	C	D	E	F	G	H	A	H	G	F	E	D	C	B	A	H
A	B	C	D	E	F	G	H	A	B	A	H	G	F	E	D	C	B	A
B	C	D	E	F	G	H	A	B	F	B	A	H	G	F	E	D	C	B
A	B	C	D	E	F	G	H	A	B	A	H	G	F	E	D	C	B	A
H	A	B	C	D	E	F	G	H	A	H	G	F	E	D	C	B	A	H
G	H	A	B	C	D	E	F	G	H	G	F	E	D	C	B	A	H	G
F	G	H	A	B	C	D	E	F	G	F	E	D	C	B	A	H	G	F
E	F	G	H	A	B	C	D	E	F	E	D	C	B	A	H	G	F	E
D	E	F	G	H	A	B	C	D	E	D	C	B	A	H	G	F	E	D
C	D	E	F	G	H	A	B	C	D	C	B	A	H	G	F	E	D	C
B	C	D	E	F	G	H	A	B	C	B	A	H	G	F	E	D	C	B
A	B	C	D	E	F	G	H	A	B	A	H	G	F	E	D	C	B	A

Page 230, Pieced Paper Quilt

contributing designers

Beth Berutich

Beth Berutich and her husband, Jim, enjoy the world of innkeeping at The Chestnut Street Inn, one of Asheville, North Carolina's historic Bed & Breakfasts (*www.chestnutstreetinn.com*). The toddler adventures of their 2-year old son, Bradley, gives Beth plenty of reasons to scrapbook countless. She also enjoys smocking and sewing heirloom children's clothing and dabbling in machine embroidery.

Rhonda Black

Rhonda Black is surrounded by creative friends and great teachers. Inspired by them and a great love of vibrant color, she dabbles in paper crafts such as card making and book binding, is an avid beader, and knits up a storm. She happily lives in Dallas, Texas.

Emily Greenelsh

Emily Greenelsh is currently a student at Tuscola High School in Waynesville, North Carolina, where she is on the tennis team. She currently has art showing at Space Out Gallery in Asheville, North Carolina.

Susan Greenelsh

Susan Greenelsh is a decorative painter and illustrator living in Waynesville, North Carolina. She believes painting and crafting are the best forms of entertainment, and that the feeling of accomplishment that comes from completing things is very exciting.

Tracy Hildebrand

Tracy Hildebrand is a glass beadmaker and jewelry artist. She makes her home in Asheville, NC and is represented by galleries throughout the southeast.

Megan Kirby

Megan Kirby followed her creative spirit when she moved from New York City to Asheville to work for Lark Books. She is a full-time art director, some-time project designer, and is always on the lookout for something new. (Hi., Elliot.)

Marthe Le Van

Marthe Le Van's painter-mom introduced her to the joys of framing at an early age. She garnered pocket money assembling metal frames and attaching hanging wires. This innocent task proved pivotal in Marthe's professional pursuits as a curator, exhibition manager, and craft designer. Marthe has created projects for several Lark books, including The Michaels book of Arts and Crafts, Simple Glass Crafts, and The Decorated Frame.

Diana Light

Diana Light lives and works in the Blue Ridge Mountains of North Carolina. After earning her B.F.A. in painting and print-making, she extended her expertise to etching and painting fine glass objects. She has contributed to numerous lark books and is the coauthor of Lark's The Weekend Crafter: Etching Glass.

Rich Maile

Rich Maile is a graphic designer living in Atlanta, Georgia. He is an unapologetic book nerd who has been known to gasp audibly upon finding a vintage copy of Stuart Little. Paradoxically, however, the vintage book is sometimes then folded into small origami boxes. Rich's other obsessions include collecting 1960s era Legion of Super Pets comics, scheming a way to meet his origami hero Tomoko Fuse and thanking his friend Dan for putting up with all of this. (A big shout out to Susan, Kris and Joan!)

Susan McBride

Susan McBride is an artist who works primarily with paper, lino-cut art and collage. She is writing and illustrating her first book for children, scheduled to be published in 2006 by Lark Books. To see more of her work, go to *susanmcbridedesign.com*.

Marie McConville

Marie McConville lives in the mountains of Western North Carolina. A longtime crafter, she specializes in card, collage, and artist book creations.

Kelly McMullen

Kelly McMullen is a graphic designer in Durham, North Carolina. Her other creative pursuits include hand-building functional and sculptural clay objects, oil painting, and gardening. Her design sensibilities combine her love of natural forms with an affinity for simplicity.

contributing designers

Suzie Millions

Suzie Millions is an artist and compulsive collector. She and her musician/artist/compulsive collector husband Lance live in an overstuffed cabin, complete with a walk-in Hank Williams shrine, in the woods of Western North Carolina. Her paintings and shrines are shown and collected extensively. See her work at **www.amerifolk.com** or contact her by email at **suziemillions@charter.net**.

Micah Pulleyn

Micah Pulleyn spent years studying book arts, papermaking, letterpress, and arts education at The Penland School of Crafts and The Iowa Center for the Book after graduating with a degree in Art History. Micah is currently an artist in residence at a new bookbinding studio and school in her home town of Asheville, North Carolina. Her fondness for handmade objects and nurturing the creative voice within fuel her lifelong passion for crafts.

Molly Smith

Molly Smith, a native Texan, is a craft designer who specializes in paper quilling. In addition to designing for a major company in the craft industry, she is working on a quilling book with Lark Books scheduled for release in spring of 2006.

Terry Taylor

Terry Taylor lends his creative spirit full time to Lark Books. In his spare time, he glues, pastes, and otherwise assembles works of art using a wide range of media from old cds to broken china. His current interests include metal jewelry. His work has been exhibited in many galleries and in many publications.

Kathryn Temple

Kathryn Temple is a celebrated visual artist and writer. She has taught art to children and is the author of Art for Kids: Drawing (Lark Books, 2005). She a contributing author to The Fire This Time: Young Activists and the New Feminism (Anchor Books, 2004.) Temple's paintings have been exhibited throughout the eastern United States and can be found in private and corporate collections throughout the country. She has been awarded artist grants and residencies.

Shannon Yokeley

Shannon Yokeley grew up in the mountains of Western North Carolina. She did her first artwork, a mural on the wall of her mother's daycare, at the age of six. Woodburning has been a hobby she's enjoyed for many years, along with horse-back riding, painting, and frequenting local flea markets for the odd piece of art.

acknowledgments

Many people contributed to the creation of this book and deserve our heartfelt thanks:

Biljana Bosevska for lending her lovely hands for how-to photography; Rain Newcomb for sharing her expertise with origami; Photographer Stewart Stokes (Asheville, North Carolina) for allowing us to reproduce the framed image on page 139; Tracy Hildebrand, Kosmos (Asheville, North Carolina), Chevron Trading and Lava (Asheville, North Carolina) for lending photography props; Colleen Kirby-Cho for support; Lauren A. Abe for photography assistance; Rhonda Black for creative input; Janet Karcasinas for logistical assistance; Rosemary Kast for her eagle eyes; all of the designers who contributed projects and technical advice; and the staff of Lark Books for so generously sharing their ideas and energy.

index